Hardscrabble

Hardscrabble

The High Cost of Free Land

DONNA E. WILLIAMS

Foreword by J. Patrick Boyer

DUNDURN
TORONTO

Editor: Laura Harris
Design: Jesse Hooper
Printer: Webcom

Library and Archives Canada Cataloguing in Publication

Williams, Donna E., author
    Hardscrabble : the high cost of free land / by Donna E. Williams ; foreword by J. Patrick Boyer.

Includes bibliographical references and index.
Issued in print and electronic formats.
ISBN 978-1-4597-0804-4 (pbk.).-- ISBN 978-1-4597-0805-1 (pdf).--ISBN 978-1-4597-0806-8 (epub)

    1. British--Ontario--Muskoka (District municipality)--History. 2. Frontier and pioneer life--Ontario--Muskoka (District municipality). 3. Ontario--Muskoka (District municipality)--Colonization. 4. British--Colonization--Ontario--Muskoka (District municipality). 5. Land settlement--Ontario--Muskoka (District municipality). 6. Muskoka (Ont. : District municipality)--History. I. Title.

FC3095.M88W55 2013   971.3'1603   C2013-900827-6
                                                C2013-900828-4

1   2   3   4   5   17   16   15   14   13

We acknowledge the support of the **Canada Council for the Arts** and the **Ontario Arts Council** for our publishing program. We also acknowledge the financial support of the **Government of Canada** through the **Canada Book Fund** and **Livres Canada Books,** and the **Government of Ontario** through the **Ontario Book Publishing Tax Credit** and the **Ontario Media Development Corporation.**

Printed and bound in Canada.

VISIT US AT
Dundurn.com | Definingcanada.ca | @dundurnpress | Facebook.com/dundurnpress

Dundurn	Gazelle Book Services Limited	Dundurn
3 Church Street, Suite 500	White Cross Mills	2250 Military Road
Toronto, Ontario, Canada	High Town, Lancaster, England	Tonawanda, NY
M5E 1M2	L41 4XS	U.S.A. 14150

~

To John, Emma, and Joe

~

Contents

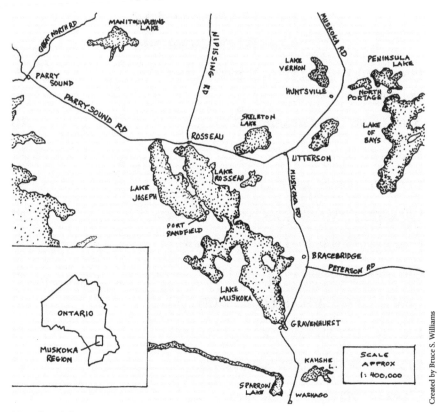

Map of Muskoka

Foreword

Creating a New World, the Hard Way

Muskoka is one of those Canadian places whose mystique extends far beyond its borders and whose renown is greater than the district's geography or population size can account for. Although some tritely refer to Muskoka today as "cottage country," a term that fails even to capture the historic depth and breadth of the district's unique vacation economy, lakeside holidays are just one component of Muskoka's story. Lumbering, agriculture, manufacturing, and vacationing have been the district's four economic pillars for a century and a half. The second of those — farming — is the lens through which Donna Williams now reveals a little-known chapter of this fascinating history. A worthy addition to the foundational stories of our country, her book's title alone, using that most apt word "hardscrabble," makes clear that farming on the Canadian Shield was not easy and the experience would shape the tough-love character of Muskokans.

In 1868, the Ontario government's offer of free land to anyone who would clear forest and create a homestead in the province's northern districts of Muskoka, Parry Sound, and Nippissing was part of a major continental contest with the United States. That country's newly formed Republican Party, whose candidate Abraham Lincoln was elected president in 1860, promoted a policy of free land for settlers as encouragement to populate the United States' "empty" frontiers. In that era the U.S. was expanding south, west, and north. The Americans had added so much new land with the purchase of Louisiana Territory from France that the country's size more than doubled. War against Mexico incorporated extensive additional territory, from Texas to California. The purchase of Alaska from Russia in the north created another American frontier. More than a few Americans believed the next acquisition should be the nearly vacant land between Alaska and the rest of the U.S. territory, which they saw being occupied merely by Aboriginals and several weak British colonies.

The momentum of its bold series of geographic expansions, when linked with the military power the United States had acquired through the Civil War, made the idea irresistible to many Americans that their "manifest destiny" was to occupy the entire North American continent. Looking north, they coveted the empty space on the map. In their eyes, it was land simply waiting to be taken.

On the Canadian side of the border, meanwhile, fear of an American push north was real. Armed raids from the United States into Canada by Fenians in the 1860s had already driven four of Britain's remaining North American colonies into a defensive political union in 1867. Despite Confederation, the risk remained real. In 1868, one of the Fathers of Confederation, D'Arcy McGee, whose bold visions for the new Canadian nation were such an inspiration to many, was assassinated in the Canadian capital by Fenian supporters. Confederation did not yet include any of the western territory, not even the epic stretch of wilderness that would later become Northwestern Ontario.

All the while, the Americans were on the ascendant in the economic life of the new Canadian nation. In addition to the northward expansion of American business, even the currency of the United States was displacing both British currency and the currency issued by private banks that was then in use. It seemed Canada would soon be absorbed into the United States, with neither a purchase agreement as was the case with sprawling Louisiana, nor a shot fired as was the case with land seized from Mexico.

One response by the Conservative government in Ottawa, to counteract the flood of American silver increasingly in use, was issuance of 25¢ bills, a paper "quarter," popularly known as a "shinplaster."

Besides dealing with the monetary challenge, a second response focused on land. Prime Minister John A. Macdonald determined that the best way to prevent the increasingly bellicose American believers in manifest destiny from occupying the open spaces of Canada was to fill them with Canadian settlers. Their presence would assert sovereignty, and their ownership would make them want to fight to protect their own farms. Into the Prairie west, as a result, went government surveyors, railway tracks, and homesteaders.

At the same time, Ontario's vast unsettled northland was impossible to defend militarily and easy for the Americans to occupy across the upper Great Lakes. The provincial government, under Premier Sandfield Macdonald, accordingly did its part in this grand strategy to thwart American incursions by dispatching homesteaders into the north. These initiatives by Canada's political leaders were neither the first nor last time in history that settlers would be pawns in a high-stakes chess game, sent into contested lands so they, rather than rivals, would inhabit the land and extend sovereignty over the territory.

Ontario's enactment of the Free Grants and Homestead Act in 1868 included the problematic "free land" incentive which some governments elsewhere also employed to populate difficult terrain that was nevertheless strategically important. In Ontario's case, free grants facilitated the crucial migration of homesteaders to Muskoka.

The northern districts were unpromising for agricultural settlement, and the government was in possession of reports by surveyors who'd returned to recommend that no farming be attempted. They saw that Muskoka's terrain, in stark contrast to land in southern Ontario, which had been cleared of trees to become productive farmland, was unsuited for agriculture because of its rock, thin soil, and swamps. Confirming that assessment, some settlers who had already taken Crown grants of land in similar terrain east of Muskoka District found themselves unable to grow crops; they spent their time writing letters to the Toronto newspapers disparaging farming on the Canadian Shield and warning others not to repeat their folly.

For higher reasons of statecraft, however, Ontario's government buried the negative reports of surveyors, disregarded the warnings of farmers, and outvoted those in the Legislature who wanted the northern lands reserved in perpetuity for Aboriginal peoples because that would have left them little populated. The government pressed on resolutely, imbued with the noble purpose of converting the northern wilderness into a homeland of settlers whose farm products would support them and whose presence would deter the Yanks.

To foster a land boom, Ontario's government and its land agents actively encouraged settlement, appealing to prospective homesteaders both in the northern United States among recent British immigrants there, and in Great Britain itself. Canadian railway companies and British shipping companies joined in to vigorously promote settlement of Ontario's new "free grant lands," knowing where their interests lay, and in expectation of future business the new population would generate.

Their message did not fall on deaf ears. Individuals struggling in cities that were industrializing and dirty, living in old places beset with problems of poverty, drunkenness, lack of work, and hunger, found the dazzling promise of free grants irresistible. Many hoped to cash in on the promise Ontario's government and its immigration agents were aggressively promoting through speeches, advertisements in American and British newspapers, and the booklet *Emigration to Canada: The Province of Ontario*, distributed widely in 1869 to publicize Muskoka's glowing agricultural prospects for new settlers.

Whatever gloom haunted their pasts, these prospective farmers positively glowed as they imagined their hundred acres of "free" land. This Muskoka dream was grounded in the belief that having one's own farm was the foundation of society and personal self-sufficiency; it promised continuation of a centuries-old pastoral way of life, an ideal far more appealing than the dystopia of heavy industry, the smudge and danger of factories, and the rawness of living in jungle-like city jumble.

Added to this free land appeal was the vision held by a number of exceptional individuals of building New Jerusalem, not just another town but a shining city on a hill, a utopia. The founding of a new society, the prospect of a better place — not in Heaven after death, but here on Earth while still alive — was the shimmering ideal for a number of religious leaders and socialists. They looked to the possibility of creating a vanguard haven in North America out of fragments, the best parts of the old, whether in places like New Harmony, Indiana, or Muskoka, Ontario.

Pioneer colonies of the devout, either escaping religious persecution or simply believing they could start over in a properly constructed Christian community, were a part of this historic migration. So were colonies founded by those resolved to flee the oppressive economic conditions of the dog-eat-dog capitalist societies and form communal and cooperative societies, where each person lived according to their needs and contributed according to their abilities.

Into this picture stepped the Reverend Styleman Herring, vicar of St. Paul's, Clerkenwell, in London, England, whose concern for overcrowded people in London and other English cities combined with his belief they could prosper in Canada. He would make the communities in England where he held sway a feeder for Muskoka settlement. That is where Donna Williams picks up the saga.

Her compelling account in *Hardscrabble*, based on extensive original research, speaks for itself. It is a true story about men and women struggling with themselves and nature. It is a case study, as well, of the complex interactions of human will and the forces of nature.

Three features of her engaging account deserve special notice. First, Donna Williams shows what this relocation program looked like from both ends — in England, and in Ontario. Often the perspective and conditions of those looking to start over in one of the settler dominions of the British Empire does not get nearly as much attention as the immigrant experience, once settlers had landed in their new country. The appeal of her book is its completeness, showing both the push *and* pull of these human dramas.

A second feature setting *Hardscrabble* apart is its treatment of how the church was part of the land settlement equation, which Donna Williams makes apparent in her portrait of the Reverend Styleman Herring. It was also intrinsic to the vision of Muskoka held by Thomas McMurray, one of the district's early settlers and first reeve elected when local government was initiated in his township. Although not an ordained clergyman like Herring, the devout Methodist was a true believer in the free grant lands as a place for people to build a better society and achieve moral uplift. Born in Scotland, McMurray settled in Ireland, married, and began a family, but hated the way the Irish were aching from famine and disease, distraught by drink, and crowded into filthy cities. Despairing of this decadent scene, he departed Ireland with his wife and children in May 1861, sailing from Londonderry straight into the promise of North America. In Muskoka, he discovered the perfect place to build New Jerusalem, and his evangelical fervour was devoted in about equal measure to the abolition of alcohol and the settlement of the free grant lands. He envisaged Muskoka and its northern neighbours of Parry Sound and Nippissing districts as a prospering homeland for *millions* of settlers — an estimate of future population shared by railway companies and land promoters in that era, perhaps not too hard to envisage with all that empty space on the map, which is exactly what salivating Americans saw, too.

Having glimpsed the future, it became McMurray's calling, like a prophet, to lead others to the promised land. Like Styleman Herring, Thomas McMurray was not passive. Seeing few new arrivals, he got the idea the government's effort to recruit homesteaders needed a more robust communications plan. So he started a newspaper, the *Northern Advocate*, the first newspaper in Ontario's northern districts, to encourage settlement by "providing practical tips from personal experience" of free grant homesteaders.

Where Styleman Herring provided the push to Muskoka, Thomas McMurray matched with the pull. His informative and appealing newspaper was widely circulated in the northern United States and especially Great Britain. The publisher hired as editor James Boyer, my great-grandfather, who as a lawyer on Broadway Avenue in New York had become "enchanted" by the prospect of free land and a new life in Muskoka. He arrived in 1869 to become not only a homesteader in Macaulay Township but municipal clerk in Bracebridge, which is the position McMurray hired him from to edit the *Advocate*. Early in 1871 they published a book to further entice settlers, entitled *The Free Grant Lands of Canada from Practical Experience of Bush Farming in the Free Grant Districts of Muskoka & Parry Sound*. The next year, working with Muskoka promoter and steamboat owner A.P. Cockburn, they invited the Canadian Press Association's editors and newspapermen for a memorable tour of Muskoka, especially enjoying a pleasant excursion through the district aboard one of Cockburn's boats. Returning to their newsrooms, the men wrote articles claiming that about three-quarters of Muskoka was good for farming, and reaffirming the gospel that the place had great agricultural capabilities.

Third and finally, most of the story of homesteaders in Canada, and certainly in Muskoka, has been told in terms of the disparate individuals and families after they reached the frontier and then hacked their homestead from the wilderness. That well-documented and accurate story is, first, one of *individualism*, and secondly, one of community — a spontaneous community formed by settlers who depended on each other, worked in bees to raise barns and skid logs to the river, and shared work of harvesting and threshing. However, there is another story.

It is the parallel tale, the one about settlers who came, not on their own, but as part of a group. This is the *collective* settlement experience, uniquely different in many respects. The individual settler had to scout the terrain to find a prospective piece of farm land, then if it was still unclaimed by others, rush to register a claim with the Crown lands agent. Those who came as part of organized settlement programs had a much different experience, from beginning to end, as Donna Williams makes clear. Rather than arriving in Canada independently, they arrived as a group, although many may have chosen to part ways soon after.

One form of organization bringing settlers to Muskoka en masse was the commercial land company, a corporate venture that was to the 1800s what a real estate developer with a plan of subdivision would be today. Another form was the settlement program for waifs from Britain's slums, back alleys, and orphanages, which was privately run by organizations such as those headed by William Quarrier, Dr. Thomas Barnardo, and others, with no government supervision. These settlement programs contributed more child labourers to Muskoka than any other section of Canada; the project to relocate England's orphans to the colony ran from 1870 to 1930 and coincided with the district's period of settlement and high demand for farm hands. A third form emanated from emigration societies such as the Reverend Styleman Herring's, as you will now discover.

Donna Williams grew fascinated with this subject years ago. We can be grateful she pursued it through a master's thesis at the University of Toronto, combed archival records, old newspapers, and parliamentary records on both sides of the Atlantic, and visited the English and Muskoka locales featured in *Hardscrabble*, in order to vividly bring this untold story to life.

Her fine book captures a past that is inseparable from what Muskoka became, and is today.

J. Patrick Boyer
Bracebridge, Muskoka
March 24, 2013

A Note on the Terminology:

Prior to the mid-1870s, "emigrant" was the predominant term used to describe both those leaving their country (in this instance, Britain or Europe), to settle elsewhere, and those arriving in a new country with intentions to settle permanently. As such, a decision has been made to retain the use of both "emigrant" and "immigrant" throughout the book.

Preface

One Saturday afternoon about nine years ago, my husband picked up a book for me from the remainder bin of the local bookstore for $4.99. *The Mice That Danced the Quadrille* was to change the course of the next several years of my life. A memoir by Thomas Osborne, it told of his family's struggles to farm a free grant of land in Ontario's Muskoka district in the mid-to-late 1870s. I was instantly curious: I knew there were farms in Muskoka, but I couldn't fathom why the government would give away free land in such a rocky part of Ontario. More research revealed that at one time, Muskoka had been subdivided into thousands of free grant lots, with an intention to create an agricultural community. I was puzzled. Who were these people who had settled Muskoka? And what had become of them? I decided then to write a book about the free grant lands, but first I had to gain some credentials.

At that time, my twin son and daughter were soon to be leaving for university, and I needed a new project to keep me occupied in my soon-to-be-empty nest. In 2005 I was accepted by the University of Toronto's master's program in history. My thesis was based on the free grants of Muskoka, but the more I researched, I found that the story wasn't just a Canadian one: in Britain many poor and unemployed people were enticed to Muskoka by emigration philanthropists to farm free land. Leading the movement was a vicar from a poor parish in the East End of London by the curious name of Styleman Herring. It seemed that Muskoka's settlement history had deep roots on both sides of the

Atlantic. After three years, I finished my degree and was anxious to turn my thesis into a book.

Many months of further research led to a first draft and, happily, to a book contract. The endeavour has been a true labour of love for me. My late father, Rudy Williams, had instilled a love of Muskoka in me from the time of my childhood; as a family, we spent many holidays roaming the back roads, visiting towns and villages, and staying in classic motels. Dad pointed out every lichen-covered rock, the misty morning lakes, and the odd abandoned log cabin. Those trips, taken during the 1950s and '60s, with me wedged in the back seat between my two big brothers, made a huge impression on me.

Hardscrabble: The High Cost of Free Land tells the story of a very different Muskoka from the one we are familiar with. While the very name Muskoka conjures up images of luxury resorts and cottages, classic boats and boathouses, as well as the spectacular lakes and waterfalls, there is a rich history of early settlement that has not been fully told. As can be expected, many of these early settlers found their land was highly unsuitable for farming, and many did not thrive. A combination of government and business interests, as well as philanthropic emigration proponents in Canada and Britain, led them to the district, and unfortunately the settlers' well-being was virtually ignored. I wrote *Hardscrabble* because I felt there was a vacuum in the tale of Muskoka settlement. While there were plenty of "hardy" pioneers in Muskoka who *did* succeed, *Hardscrabble* honours the ones who never had a chance.

Chapter One

Free Grant Fever

The shades of night were falling as we reached Bracebridge. The moon rose above the great pine trees, and made a wide pathway of silver across the dark waters. Near the landing-stage, a mass of blazing pine-logs revealed the black shadows of the surrounding woods, and flecked the waters below with red and gold. [1]
— Charles Marshall, *The Canadian Dominion*

As the steamer *Wenonah* slid toward the Bracebridge wharf on the evening of September 14, 1870, the townspeople gathered to greet their distinguished guests with blazing bonfires and three resounding cheers, for this was no ordinary party of passengers. Aboard the side-wheel paddle steamer was a delegation of dignitaries who had travelled more than one hundred miles north of Toronto to Muskoka to see Ontario's free grant district firsthand. Among them were John Sandfield Macdonald, the premier and attorney general of Ontario; John Carling, commissioner of public works and brewing mogul; Stephen Richards, commissioner of Crown lands; Thomas McMurray, local reeve, businessman, and avid Muskoka booster; and A.P. Cockburn, Muskoka navigation pioneer and politician. Joining this party of "celebrities," as McMurray later referred to them, were two guests from England: Charles Marshall, an author and journalist; and the Reverend A. Styleman Herring, the vicar of a poor parish in East End London, an emigration enthusiast, and free grant advocate. The rousing welcome these gentlemen received in this little town in the Muskoka bush was just the kick-off to an evening of self-congratulatory merriment.

The gentlemen disembarked the *Wenonah* and headed toward the village centre by way of Manitoba Street, past the roaring waters of the Bracebridge Falls. They were sure to have savoured the indescribably intoxicating scent of Muskoka, redolent of pine and lichen, and, in mid-September, the tangy aroma of autumn as leaves began to change colour, foretelling of wintry nights ahead. With the help of a second bonfire lighting up the main street, they would perceive a scattering of small dwellings and commercial properties — harbingers of Bracebridge's potential. The men finally reached the Dominion House, a welcome sight after their long journey by rail, steamer, and stage wagon. The party poured through the hotel doors for a banquet prepared for fifty to sixty people. Thomas McMurray diligently recorded the proceedings for his newspaper, the *Northern Advocate*, and later published them in his *Free Grant Lands of Canada* guide to the district. Thanks to McMurray, we are able to join the revellers as they gathered on this fine Muskoka evening. Throughout the festivities, while sampling the free-flowing supply of ale and wine, this very masculine gathering toasted all and sundry: they raised their glasses to Queen Victoria; the governor general and lieutenant governors of the Dominion of Canada; the army and navy; the Ontario government; the emigration societies of "old England"; the Toronto, Simcoe and Muskoka Junction Railway; the free grant district; and last but not least, they exuberantly toasted one another.

John Teviotdale, a local reeve, storekeeper, and postmaster, chaired the occasion, and, as Charles Marshall observed, "speeches, patriotic, and humorous, and explanatory, and promissory" were made.[2] One by one, hosts and guests alike rose and addressed the room. First to speak was Premier John Sandfield Macdonald, who headed up a Liberal-Conservative coalition government that had introduced the opening of the free grant district just two years before. He assured his listeners that his party's interest in the free grant lands was not political, but rather, driven by its dedication to the people themselves, and implied that funds were to be made available to further Muskoka's chance at prosperity. Next, Stephen Richards, the main architect of the free grant scheme, and the

Conservative representing the riding of Niagara, somewhat pompously apologized for not having previously visited Muskoka — "his duties, public and private, were so enormous that he found it impossible to get away."[3] Richards's short speech was followed by Styleman Herring's, the vicar of St. Paul's, Clerkenwell, in London, who responded to the toast to England's emigration societies with a wish that the overcrowded population of England could find prosperity in Canada. After more tributes, Thomas McMurray thanked the government for improvements that had been made in the district since his arrival in 1861, while boldly reminding those present there were still issues to be solved. He suggested that settlers should not have to pay a duty to the government on timber they had felled, that settlers who had purchased land prior to the free grant policy should not be held in arrears if they could not pay debts, and that new registry offices were needed in Bracebridge. Speeches carried on throughout the long evening, with Charles Marshall assuring the assembly that he believed Canada had a great future. The final toast was made to "our American Cousins," responded to by a Mr. Barker, correspondent for the *Springfield Republican*. The celebration concluded with patriotic zeal. "God Save the Queen" was sung, followed by three cheers for Her Majesty Queen Victoria. The Dominion House had obviously served the government's guests well: the festivities didn't wind down until two o'clock in the morning.

An impressive evening, indeed. But as in all public relations events, the veneer is what counts; the inner truth can be less palatable. This boisterous banquet was not merely a celebration of the free grant lands of Muskoka, but a wholesale effort by the Canadian contingent to counter criticism of a land settlement scheme that showed early signs of fraying at the edges. The Canadian hosts were savvy operators. There was no record of disgruntled settlers among the guests; perhaps a few were lurking in the shadows outside, barred from this likely invitation-only event. It was in the hosts' interest to woo Marshall and Herring. The former went on to write a glowing account of the free grant lands in his book *The Canadian Dominion*, published the following year; the latter would focus on Muskoka as a destination for the members of his London emigration society. Muskoka would have been relatively easy to sell as an agricultural destination — an almost virgin landscape of pine and deciduous forests, glittering lakes, impressive waterfalls — a virtual paradise for aspiring settlers. But there was a serpent in this alleged Garden of Eden, one that Muskoka boosters strove hard to downplay — rock. Located on the Canadian Shield, Muskoka is replete with Precambrian outcrops, some encrusted with thin, acidic soil, others boldly exposed to the elements. During the evening's banquet — according to McMurray's account, that is — nothing was said about this obvious road-block to the district's agricultural success. The sublime landscape, coupled with the Canadians' enthusiastic endorsements of Muskoka, clouded the judgement of both Herring and Marshall, and the myth of the free grant scheme's viability was perpetuated for the time being. Did Macdonald or Richards, McMurray or Cockburn, have any misgivings for perhaps pulling the wool over these men's eyes? Unfortunately, the architects of the free grant scheme could not plead ignorance — the suitability of land on the Canadian Shield for agricultural settlement had been the subject of fierce debate for the past several decades.

~

Free land grants, or offers of cheap land, were not a new phenomenon. They have been used throughout history as a means of fulfilling a country's "manifest destiny," whether within a country, as in the United States, or as a means to successfully colonize far-flung regions, as was the case in Great Britain. However, such schemes have frequently had dire results. Decades before Ontario's free grant legislation, Western Australia's Swan River colony, founded in 1829 by British naval captain James Stirling, was colonized — partly in order to prevent France from claiming the land for itself. The settlement, which was soon christened Perth, was billed as an agrarian paradise for settlers, but the emigrants who arrived at the colony hoping for cheap land found poor soil and an inhospitable climate. As a result, the extra land granted to settlers who brought extended family and servants proved insufficient for sustaining large numbers of people. Perhaps bitter at the failure of the settlement, Stirling, in the same spirit as many Muskoka free grant advocates, blamed the settlers themselves for the colony's failure, claiming they were unsuccessful because they were inefficient farmers with unrealistic expectations. Eventually, over the next decades, convict labour boosted the population, and with the discovery of gold in Western Australia, the economy gradually grew.

The architects of empire and nation building, however, rarely learn from past experience. Many years after the Swan River fiasco, settlers in the United States were enticed by Abraham Lincoln's Homestead Act of 1862, blithely heading west to farm the vast prairies, where poor soil, drought, extreme weather, and plagues of locusts discouraged many. In a move to equalize opportunity, the Act specified that land grants should be 160 acres each, yet these small parcels of land were inadequate to support the farmers who settled them, and prosperity was elusive. When the transcontinental railway reached the west coast in 1869, a measure of prosperity was achieved, as settlers could enjoy the boost in the economy brought on by improved transportation. However, in the initial years of these American and Australian settlements, the settlers bore the brunt of hardship as they carved out a living in a frequently hostile environment. As well, the Aboriginal populations suffered as they were supplanted from their own land, sometimes violently. Ironically, the Indigenous people were much better equipped for survival on the land that had sustained them for generations.

If free grant schemes from the past were not very successful, what possessed legislators to copy the idea in Muskoka?

Such schemes had been attempted in Upper Canada, as well as in Atlantic Canada, as early as the eighteenth century. In Upper Canada, these early settlement schemes were initiated in order to reward military personnel and newly arrived United Empire Loyalists, who had travelled north from the United States, preferring to live in a Crown colony rather than a newly independent republic. At this time, the grants were located in the less-rugged parts of southern Ontario, while the northern expanses of the province were intended to be reserved for the Aboriginal population. These land grants were often not successfully farmed, however, and merely held in speculation. As a result, the land was not worked agriculturally as intended, but held till rising land values could be exploited and a profit made. When these early schemes failed to encourage settlement, the government abandoned the concept for the next few decades.

Settlement schemes were not just conducted by the government in Ontario's early years. Two notable projects had some similarities, although they were initiated in opposite ends of the province. Thomas Talbot, an Anglo-Irish military man, was private secretary to John Graves

Simcoe, Upper Canada's first lieutenant governor, from 1792 to 1794. After spending a few years in Britain, he returned to Canada, and, in 1803, was granted land in southwestern Ontario for purposes of founding a settlement. Talbot's settlers began arriving a few years after, and they were promised legal possession of their land if they actually cleared and cultivated it, and built a house. Initially, Talbot's settlement was quite successful: among his achievements was to encourage settlers to build roads throughout the district, most notably, the Talbot Road, and to encourage the land's cultivation by suppressing land speculation. However, Talbot's powers eventually diminished: the province wished to take over the running of the settlement, partly due to Talbot's eccentricities and rather despotic attitude toward his settlers. As well, there was a growing backlash against the Family Compact, the wealthy, well-entrenched Anglican establishment that had administered the province for the past decades, and with whom Talbot highly identified.

Despotic tendencies led to the downfall of Archibald McNab, as well. As chief of the clan McNab in his native Scotland, he came in 1822 to Canada to escape debts, and soon after founded a settlement on the Ottawa River. Scottish settlers arrived soon after, but again, power went to McNab's head, and he ran his community as if it were a sort of feudal kingdom. Settlers rebelled for years, until in the 1840s, the government stepped in and McNab was removed from his own settlement. Both Talbot's and McNab's endeavours demonstrated that emigration schemes such as theirs were unlikely to survive when left to the whims of leaders with little accountability.

By the mid-1800s, southern Ontario had seen a rapid population growth: prosperous towns were enjoying a healthy economy, and, as agricultural land had long been under cultivation, vacant land was scarce and established farms were expensive for those with little capital. Immigration was being promoted as a means to further expand the country's population, and these new citizens would need a place to settle. In 1852, William Lyon Mackenzie and Joseph Hartman (members of the Reform Party, founded in 1832) addressed the Legislative Assembly, requesting surveys be made into the Ottawa-Huron tract, in the hope of settling the district for young

Canadians and emigrants. Their plea was not in vain, for shortly after, a network of colonization roads was initiated in northeastern Ontario. The first was the Ottawa-Opeongo, begun in the early 1850s. The road snaked west from the Ottawa region but was never completed; it failed even to reach Lake Opeongo, about halfway to its intended destination of Georgian Bay. Settlers, many of them emigrants from Great Britain, were granted one hundred acres of land adjacent to the road. But there were those who conceded that the area may not be everyone's cup of tea. An 1857 Department of Agriculture emigration pamphlet contained some unusually frank advice for the emigrant accustomed to the relatively tamer topography of Britain. "The Canadian Government [has] ... no desire to encourage emigration to this Colony by sanctioning fancy sketches of rural felicity, or by permitting hopes of prosperity that cannot be completely realised to be held out.... [The settlers] must not estimate the value of land here by the standard that obtains in the parent kingdom."[4] Although couched in rather twee Victorian prose, the pamphlet certainly hit the nail on the head. The Opeongo Road was hardly a region of "rural felicity": it was isolated in the extreme, with a rugged terrain and harsh winter weather conditions — not exactly the Sussex countryside. By the early 1860s, these early free grant schemes, however shaky, came into direct competition with the British-based Canadian Land and Emigration Company, which was selling land cheaply in the Haliburton area, which is situated just east of Muskoka. The company's settlers were rather disconcerted that free land was being offered in other parts of Ontario, and they petitioned the government — unsuccessfully, as it turned out — for compensation.

However, the competition was short-lived. Haliburton proved to be isolated and infertile, and the Canadian Land and Emigration Company struggled with its settlement for years to come. Considering the failure of these early settlement schemes, the government was perhaps even more determined that Muskoka would be a success. In 1856, the district was opened for settlement, and construction of the Muskoka Road began shortly after. By 1859, free grants of one hundred acres adjacent to the road were offered to prospective settlers. A stipulation required these settlers to contribute labour for the road's upkeep. And yet, before long, warnings that the district may not be ideal for agriculture were expressed.

In a report on the Muskoka Road in 1862, land agent R.J. (Richard Jose) Oliver noted, "The race now existing between the United States and ourselves for securing the tide of Emigration demands our most serious attention … care must be taken that discouraging accounts shall not be sent home to those of their friends who intend to follow."[5] His words were proof that "discouraging reports" were rampant long before the Free Grants Act was passed, but the government chose largely to ignore them.

~

On January 9, 1868, two years prior to the Dominion House banquet in Bracebridge, members of the provincial Parliament took their seats at three in the afternoon in the old Ontario Legislature building on Toronto's Front Street, between John and Simcoe. Top of the agenda that day was the government's proposal to offer free grants to settlers across the Ottawa-Huron tract, most specifically in the Muskoka district.[6] The ensuing debate was passionate: those endorsing free grants were convinced that mistakes of the past would not be repeated; the detractors perhaps had more knowledge of those failed schemes and were equally adamant that this present scheme should be abandoned, or at least altered for the benefit of the settlers.

The government was, however, optimistic that with firm stipulations against speculation in place, success was guaranteed. In its favour, Muskoka had the advantage of being relatively easier to access than other regions of the Ottawa-Huron tract, and a rudimentary transportation network — road, water, and rail — was already in the works. As well, a good deal of money had already been spent on surveying the land. To gain a firm understanding of the optimism, and of the skepticism, that was voiced that day, we will join these honourable members as they take their seats and the debate over the free grants begins.[7]

Minutes after the commencement of the three o'clock session, John Charles Rykert, the Conservative party member for Lincoln County, addressed John Stevenson, the Speaker of the House, demanding that the government of the day, John Sandfield Macdonald's Liberal-Conservative coalition, be a little more forthcoming about its intention to open the "wild lands" of Ontario for free grant agricultural settlement. He reminded the House that in the past decade emigrants had been induced to wild lands in other parts of the province, which also lay on the Canadian Shield, with disastrous results. "If [an 1863] report could be believed," the *Globe* quoted him, "much of the land on which emigrants had settled was totally unfit — a good deal of suffering and hardship, if not of starvation, had been endured by some — and the tide of emigration had long ago turned from their shores to the United States." Rykert was concerned that the Ottawa-Huron tract was once again to be opened up for free grant settlement, and was anxious that prior mistakes were not repeated, as many earlier settlers on poor land had abandoned their homes. He demanded that the government report on exactly how much arable land there was in these newly proposed free grant lands. A particular concern was that the Macdonald government was proposing that settlers could not sell the lumber they cleared on their land, but must relinquish it to the government or pay the same dues that actual lumber companies paid. They could, however, keep the timber that was felled strictly for clearing purposes — that is, with the intent of cultivation — for fuel, and for the erection of buildings and fences.

Rykert's concerns sparked a heated debate that day in the House. Premier John Sandfield Macdonald, the Conservative member for Cornwall, was quick to jump into the fray, countering Rykert's accusation that the free grant district was unfit for agriculture. He explained that it was impossible to calculate how much land was arable, and that the settlers who had abandoned their homes in the past had not been "actual" settlers; they had only taken residence for the time it took to cut and sell the lumber on their land. Frederick William Cumberland, Conservative member for Algoma, found it difficult to believe that Macdonald couldn't calculate the amount of arable land in the free grant district; he reminded the government of the considerable expense that both pre- and post-Confederation governments had spent on surveyors over the past several years. Macdonald shot back that it would take years to go over the land "lot by lot, and acre by acre," but did agree that earlier free grant schemes had been complete failures. As for the timber issue, he suggested that by relinquishing their rights to the timber to the government, the settlers would avoid direct taxation — after all, the government was entitled to raise revenues on the land in some way. And as far as the mistakes of years gone past, his government could not be held responsible for errors made by previous governments. A.P. (Alexander Peter) Cockburn, the Liberal member for Victoria North, had financial interests in Muskoka, with his navigation company and general store in Gravenhurst. He disputed Rykert's earlier warnings, claiming that lumbermen were never allowed on settlers' lands and that there was no question of the district's suitability for agriculture, as it was well known that good land bore the best timber.

Claims and counterclaims were bandied about the House that day. Thomas Scott, Conservative member for Grey North, pointed out that white pine lands often proved to be poor agricultural districts once the lumber was felled, and backed up his opinion by referring to an 1863 Parliamentary Committee report that found pine land not suited for agriculture. He also reminded the Speaker that the Opeongo colonization road had all but been abandoned due to poor soil. Rykert, perhaps sensing the issue was getting out of hand, assured the House he had not been blaming the present government for past misfortunes, but insisted past surveyors' reports should be taken into consideration. He pointed out that not all of these reports had been favourable as to the land's fitness for cultivation, and, most significantly, that surveyors who presented an unfavourable report on the proposed agricultural areas in the Ottawa-Huron tract were never hired for a second job. Henry Smith, Conservative member for Frontenac, suggested that settlers must know the condition of the land before they take possession, and they should be entitled to the lumber on it. He suggested that the free grant lands should be divided into two parts: one solely for agriculture, the other for lumber interests. As well, he was in favour of a homestead exemption law, which would provide poor settlers protection from creditors. In conclusion, Smith warned that perhaps the government should hold off on the free grant legislation until the actual amount of arable land had been determined. And so the debate continued: some members urging caution regarding the free grants, others advocating swift passing of the bill. Finally, Macdonald announced that Stephen Richards would look further into the matter and return with his resolutions.

Presumably, over the next few weeks, Richards retreated with his advisers to discuss the objections made to the free grant proposal. In the meantime, politicians were not the only ones concerned with the new settlement scheme. On January 20, 1868, the *Globe* printed a lengthy letter to the editor from "Backwoodsman" in Peterborough. The settler made a series of observations about land settlement in the districts north of the settled areas on the eastern edge of Lake Ontario. "Where the land is covered with pine, or pine and hemlock, with very little hard wood, as a rule it is little else than a succession of rocky knolls and beaver ponds, and ... is almost totally unfit for settlement." He conceded that there was some good land, but "[A] serious obstacle to settlement, however, is that these tracts of good land are often separated from each other — perhaps for miles — by tracts of broken, rocky and, of course, worthless lands over which it is difficult to make and sustain roads." He echoed Henry Smith's suggestion that lumbermen and settlers should have access to separate tracts of land: the settlers wouldn't suffer because timber lands were poor for agricultural purposes. "Backwoodsman" disagreed with those in the House who disparaged the colonization roads, explaining that they could be improved with a network of smaller byways that would help settlers reach suitable land.

"Backwoodsman" struck a nerve with Crown lands agent R.J. Oliver, who countered the settler's observations on January 28, reminding readers that he himself had been a location agent when the first grants along the Muskoka Road were being given out in 1859, and since then the community had prospered. Oliver was a major free grant proponent — after all, his job depended on the success of the scheme. He added a postscript: "There is an extensive district of good agricultural land contiguous to this [the Muskoka] road."

Oliver seems to have been rather sensitive about the letter from "Backwoodsman," and yet perhaps he had reason, for doubts concerning the scheme were being aired even before the bill's first reading. A January 22 editorial in the *Globe* chastised Stephen Richards for being too "niggardly" with the free grant stipulations. It gently ridiculed him for repeatedly asserting that Ontario's free grant scheme was much more liberal than that of the United States. Continuing on, the editorial insisted that there must be, as in the United States, a homestead exemption law in place to protect settlers from creditors. Furthermore, providing settlers pay their dues, mineral and timber rights should be given to them. The fact that these concerns about the quality of free grant land and the settlement itself were being expressed by legislators, settlers, and newspaper editors is significant: the scheme was already under question even before being formally introduced to the Legislature.

Richards presented the free grant bill on Friday, January 24, for its first reading, just after the session's commencement at three o'clock in the afternoon. Each of the six resolutions was debated in the House and the discussions that ensued were at times partisan, but also presented with a deal of mutual respect that seems to have long since gone out of fashion. Most members, no matter their political affiliation, were determined to emerge from the Legislature with a free grant scheme that benefitted all players. The deliberations during a session that carried on till almost midnight reveal that the Act was thoughtfully constructed and subjected to careful scrutiny, yet it soon becomes evident that the architects of the plan, as well as those in dissent, continually skirted the most important issue — the preponderance of rock in the district.

Before Richards addressed the House, Henry Smith asked if the Act would allow settlers to acquire timber rights on their land, before receiving patent on it. Again, Richards indicated he would not make that concession. At that point, the House went into committee with William Lount, Liberal member for Simcoe North, assigned as the chair. The first of six resolutions was carried quickly: the province should offer free grants of land to "develop the agricultural resources of the Province." Richards's second resolution was also passed almost immediately, as it simply delineated the geographical area of the free grants — broadly speaking, the land that spread across the Ottawa-Huron tract. There was a short debate over the third resolution, which stated that any head of household or person eighteen years or older could acquire a free grant that would not exceed one hundred acres. Alexander David Ferrier, Conservative member from Wellington Centre, asked if "person" included females as well as males. Richards rather primly assured him that he "wished to allow ladies an opportunity of getting these grants," which was followed by shouts of "hear, hear." Married women were given the right to own property in Upper Canada in 1859, so this decision is not surprising. The third resolution was carried.

The fourth resolution, which set out the structure of the Act, stated that the settler would be entitled to a patent on the land (which means he would then own it) if he or she had maintained five years of "continual and actual residence," had cleared not less than fifteen acres, and had built a house no smaller than sixteen by twenty feet in dimension. The settler was required to clear at least two acres per year. Henry Smith argued that "continual and actual" was too stringent. Would the settler lose ownership of the land if he had to seek employment elsewhere if the family was in need? Richards assured him that an absence of six months per year would be allowed. After discussion among the members, the fourth resolution was carried. As we have seen, the term "actual settler" is key to the Free Grants Act, as it demonstrates the intention to discourage speculation on the land: this time, Ontario was offering free land specifically for agricultural settlement and the government was determined not to repeat past free grant scheme failures.

The fifth resolution was the most controversial, as it brought up two issues. First of all, John Sandfield Macdonald stipulated that in order to ensure that the settler stayed on the land and was able to improve it, he wouldn't be held for any debts for twenty years from the date of location. Secondly, the settler couldn't sell or give away that land for the first five years, at which time he would receive a patent for the land. These stipulations were set to ensure the settlers' continued occupation of the land, and to protect them from creditors. Another lively debate ensued. Edward Blake, Liberal member for Bruce South, asked if an "alienee," someone who took over the land from the original settler after the patent was given, would be given the same protections. Richards replied with a concise "Yes" and Edmund Burke Wood, the provincial treasurer and Conservative member for Brant South, replied, "Certainly not." Blake couldn't resist a dig. Amid laughter, he replied, "'Yes,' says the Commissioner; 'No,' says the Treasurer; what says the Government?" Blake didn't believe it was necessary to extend the exemption to the land after it passed out of a settler's hands. Macdonald explained that the exemption only applied to the original settler, not to further patentees; Blake then demanded that the resolution be amended.

As the afternoon wore on, members offered suggestions on improving the all-important issue of settlers' land alienation rights — which is the act of passing the land on to another. Matthew Crooks Cameron, Conservative member for Toronto East, argued against restrictions once a patent was issued. "It was true, a man might mortgage and squander his property, but it was impossible to legislate against the acts of the improvident." Henry Smith rather paternalistically replied that "the principal of the homestead law was to protect the property of the improvident man against his improvident acts, and keep it in the hands of his family." Finally, after much discussion, Richards proposed an amendment that the exemption would only apply to the settler and his family and heirs, and the land could not be alienated before the patent was received. Blake replied by suggesting that *all* bona fide settlers across the province should receive the protection of the homestead exemption, not just those who were about to settle the free grants. Further discussion revealed that many of the early settlers in Ontario who had paid for their plot on public lands were in arrears; certainly it would be cruel for these settlers not to receive the same concessions as the new settlers the government was now trying to attract with free grants. This echoed Thomas McMurray's comment at the Dominion House banquet two years before. Macdonald replied that there was no cruelty in asking men to fulfill their bargains, but he had a fund set aside to aid distressed settlers. Finally the House recessed at six o'clock; presumably a dinner break was in order.

Blake returned after the recess with a new amendment that would allow settlers and their heirs on ungranted lands — that is, land they had purchased from the government — an exemption from debt for the twenty years that followed the passing of the bill. Macdonald strongly objected: this would be detrimental to the free grant scheme. After much debate, Blake withdrew his amendment and the fifth resolution was carried. At this point, the sixth and final resolution was read out by Richards. He stated that free grant locations should only be made on lands suitable for actual settlement and cultivation, not on lands suitable for timber or mineral resources. He also stipulated that all valuable timber, mines, and minerals on that land should be reserved for the government. Another hot-button issue, the timber rights came under intense scrutiny. John McMurrich, Liberal member for York South, asked why settlers and lumbermen could not be kept apart so that they would have absolutely no contact with each other, thereby avoiding any conflicts. Apart from that, he agreed that settlers should not have rights to the lumber on their land. Macdonald assured the House that land agents were quite capable of distinguishing between settlers who intended to cultivate the land from those who wished to use it for timber or mineral purposes. Should a settler cut more timber than he needed, he should pay lumber dues. Members weighed in with various opinions until, to the amusement of the House, A.J. Cockburn claimed that thus far no one was really getting the point. He insisted on an amendment that would give settlers timber rights, agreeing with Macdonald that it would be a simple matter for land agents to distinguish between a bona fide settler and an aspiring lumberman. John Lorn McDougall, Liberal member for Renfrew South, suggested that settlers should be able to cut timber during the winter months when land wasn't under cultivation; this would give them a profitable occupation. Finally, Cockburn's amendment was put to the House and was defeated. Blake suggested that the resolution must be altered to make clear that the settler could have his timber after he had fulfilled the terms of his grant, and Macdonald agreed to this amendment. The resolution was then carried, and the session was adjourned at eleven-forty-five in the evening.

The free grant bill was presented to the House on Friday, January 31, for a second reading. After a short discussion, the members decided it best to wait until the following Monday, when members of the Legislature were in full attendance, before voting on it. And yet on February 3, the debate continued, probably to the consternation of Stephen Richards, who must have at this point thought the whole matter settled. The first six resolutions were immediately adopted, and added clauses were then debated. Most of the arguments, both pro and con, had already been covered in previous sessions, but a few vital objections were still being raised, most specifically the contentious timber and mineral rights issue. Thomas Roberts Ferguson, Conservative member from Simcoe South, rather cleverly pointed out that if a settler wasn't allowed timber rights on the trees he had cleared until his five years' settlement period had ended, then he would have no incentive to clear his land until then. If he cleared, for example, thirty acres the first year, he would be charged timber dues. Sensing, perhaps, the irony of such a situation, Timothy Blair Pardee, the Liberal member for Lambton, asked what would happen if the settler simply burned his wood upon cutting it. Richards replied, in what must have seemed illogical even to him, that then he wouldn't have to pay dues on the timber. In their desperation to avoid timber speculation, the government had resorted to a ridiculous policy that sanctioned wastage of timber in order to keep the benefit away from the settler.

Archibald McKellar, Liberal member for Bothwell, obviously exasperated, suggested the whole bill was wrong in principle. In the first place, he boldly reminded the House that the free grant land was not good for agricultural purposes, an aspect of the scheme that few were willing to address. Secondly, he disagreed totally with the government's stand on timber and mineral rights: "The Government took what was on the earth, and what was in the bowels of the earth. What they held out to the settler as a free grant, was but a phantom." The entire bill was "a twopenny halfpenny policy," he added. After more verbal jousting, some of it becoming slightly more congenial, Donald Sinclair, Liberal member from Bruce North, echoed McKellar's sentiments. He suggested that if the free grant lands were the best lands in the province, then timber dues might make sense, but as the land was inferior and most likely would be settled by the poor, why restrict their chances at gaining a livelihood? Unfortunately, and to the detriment of future settlers, his remarks were not picked up on, and the final resolution of the bill was agreed upon. The following day, on February 4, the free grant bill was given a third reading. Surprisingly, Richards had made a small concession, deciding to give settlers mineral rights, after all. His grudging concession was met with shouts of "hear, hear." Henry Smith, pushing his luck, rather mischievously suggested that as Richards was in such a good humour, why not let them keep the timber, too. Macdonald answered "no, no," and finally the bill was passed on the third reading.

On February 6, the *Globe* ran an editorial concerning the free grant scheme. "Bit by bit, slowly and painfully, Ministers yielded to the advice of more enlightened men, and abandoned or modified several of the many restrictions with which the scheme was burdened." On a slightly more positive note, the *Globe* was delighted to announce that Richards had generously conceded that the settler could make use of or sell rock from quarries on his land immediately upon arrival, not when the patent came up in five years. The editorial complained of the stingy nature of the Act, especially concerning timber rights, and warned that "the Province is as much under obligation to the settler as the settler is to the Province." All in all, the paper endorsed the Act, suggesting that flaws could be ironed out in the future.

Just three days before the Free Grants and Homestead Act was passed, on February 25, the *Globe* featured a letter to the editor on its front page. "Poor Settler," as the correspondent identified himself, was a farmer from

Bracebridge, and he hoped to catch Stephen Richards's attention. He expressed his and his neighbours' dissatisfaction with the free grant lands, and he didn't mince words:

> Indeed several people are wanting to petition the Washington Government for a free passage to their lands, and leave the country altogether. A farmer living in the neighbourhood of Toronto or London has no idea of this country.... Rocky ridges running like parallels of latitude cut up the whole country, so that a lot may have a ridge across the front, middle or back end.... And this is the paradise that Mr. Richards is so afraid of giving too much away. Did he ever see this part of Ontario, or is he, as the popular notion of him here is, a lawyer, whose knowledge of agriculture is confined to drawing deeds and transfers of land.

Bitter at the pine being taken from the settlers, he added, "Did Mr. Richards ever read in his Bible 'Blessed is the man who considereth the poor?'"

Perhaps Richards read his Tuesday paper with some trepidation that day. "Poor Settler" proved to be quite perceptive. Richards *was* a lawyer, a Queen's Counsel, no less. And as he was to admit to his Dominion House audience two years later, he had *not* visited Muskoka prior to that occasion, as he had been *too busy* with his *enormous* duties, public and personal. How could he have sanctioned settlement on land he had never seen? There had been plenty of warnings that Muskoka was unsuited for agriculture, many from the surveyors of past decades. Unfortunately, Richards hadn't taken it upon himself to see if those warnings were justified.

On February 28, 1868, An Act to Secure Free Grants and Homesteads to Actual Settlers on the Public Lands was passed in the presence of Henry William Stisted, the lieutenant governor. The ceremony began at six o'clock, when Stisted arrived to give royal assent not only to the free grant bill, but to several other bills as well. He was met by a guard of honour, with one hundred members of the Thirteenth Hussars and one hundred of the Seventeenth Regiment. A military band played as he approached the Legislature. It was a much grander occasion than the much more down-to-earth gathering at the Dominion House a few years later, but one that held similar ironies. For the men who gathered with much pomp and circumstance at the Legislature were engaging in a similar exercise as the collection of "celebrities" at the Dominion House — celebrating a settlement scheme that would have a major impact on the lives of other people. As Donald Sinclair had bluntly suggested, the Free Grants Act would put poor people on unfit land — and poor people throughout history have rarely had a voice in their own affairs.

Spring comes late to the Muskoka district, and so it was not until April that Stephen Richards announced that the free grant lands were open for settlement. But first, Richards had offered some concessions that might draw further interest to the free grant lands. He assured the Legislature that as there were no timber licences granted for the area, there would be no danger of conflicts between the settlers and lumbermen. As well, settlers who wished to farm more than their allotted one hundred acres could purchase an additional one hundred for fifty cents per acre, but must follow the original conditions of the Free Grants Act — except for the requirement of building a home. Richards's announcement may have appeased some critics — at least settlers would have an opportunity to improve their chance of success if their original one hundred acres was unsuited for cultivation.

Over the summer months and into the autumn, as settlers began to trickle into the Muskoka district, the debate over the free grant scheme seemed to have momentarily died down, probably because it was too early to assess its success. However, in December 1868, Richards was again attacked for his determination that settlers who had purchased their land prior to the free grants and who were in arrears be held for payment. This rather echoed Edward Blake's protest in the early debates over the Act: he had stressed that it was ridiculous to dole out free land in one part of the province while holding those settlers on ungranted land accountable for debt often accrued because of the poor agricultural quality of their soil. It did seem illogical to have some settlers enjoying free land and being exempt from debt, while others were struggling to pay off land they had bought prior to the Act. Perhaps because he was facing continual criticism, Richards made an astonishing gesture of conciliation. He announced to the Legislature that free grant settlers would now be given two hundred acres, considering that some land was so poor that only half of what a settler received was cultivatable. Extra land was granted if a settler's land was particularly rocky. It was a significant admission of partial defeat: likely he hoped to keep the critics at bay for the time being. This motion was passed and the amendment was carried on January 23, 1869.

But before the passing of that amendment, on December 10, 1868, the desirability of encouraging emigration as a means to populate the free grant lands was hotly debated in the House. John Lorn McDougall complained that there were few emigrants in the free grant lands of eastern Ontario. Stephen Richards assured the House that Muskoka was the main focus for emigration to the settlement at this time, so that wasn't really an issue, and in time, he would turn his attention to other areas of the province. Yet Henry Dolphus Smith, Liberal member for Leeds, informed the House that he'd recently met with a young man who had travelled through Muskoka and claimed that the settlers there were all anxious to sell their land. Smith remarked that "people were not usually so anxious to get quit of a really good thing." Fellow Liberal William Beatty, from Bruce South, was astonished at such a "sweeping assertion," and Smith defended himself, saying that he meant the land was not suited for *foreign* emigration. Beatty acknowledged Smith's backing down on the issue, to which Smith replied, "Not a bit of it." And so the bickering continued.

∾

The most significant aspect of the December debates was the admission by Richards that the land was so poor that an extra one hundred acres was being thrown in to sweeten the deal. Time and again, we shall see how Muskoka's verdant forests might have fooled the visitors into thinking the land was arable. But no one who visits the district today, or who did in the late 1860s, can deny that the district's most distinctive feature is the Canadian Shield. The surface of the Shield that we see today is the result of the movement of ancient glaciers that cut swaths through the landscape, exposing the ancient bedrock beneath and cutting out basins for the region's many lakes. The Shield becomes hidden by "cover rock" (much younger, softer rock) and by a thin veneer of soil and glacial deposits at the Severn River, Muskoka's southern border, which is why the landscape changes so dramatically as one heads north from that point. In some places the rock's smooth surface virtually paves the ground; in others, it dominates the landscape, rising metres above the roads that have been cut through it. The soil is thin and acidic, and, except for a few clay pockets, most in the Bracebridge area, it is not suitable for sustained agriculture. As we have learned from the Legislature debates, early surveyors had reported on the preponderance of rock in Muskoka; unfortunately, their conclusions were not always consistent.

The surveyors' early forays into the Canadian Shield were feats of incredible endurance. Admittedly, the term *surveyor* hardly conjures up the romanticism of early fur traders or voyageurs, whose early exploits in the Canadian wilderness have become legendary. Yet these men should be counted among the heroes of Canadian history: they fought appalling conditions, enduring extreme temperatures, blackflies, and disagreeable terrain covered with endless swamps and undergrowth. Injuries were common, scurvy was a threat, and budgets were low, frequently forcing the men to face starvation. Alexander Shirreff, who surveyed much of the Ottawa-Huron tract in 1829, advocated settlement in Muskoka early on. He admitted that there were extremely rocky areas in some parts of the district, but concluded that "[t]he central part, however, of this wide region is, without doubt, generally good, there being ... every reason to suppose that the soil increases in fertility as we descend from the elevated tracts on the head waters of the Nesswabic and Muskoka, toward lake Nipissing." [8]

Robert Bell's survey in 1847 was guardedly optimistic, which is somewhat surprising, for his party endured terrible weather conditions and near starvation during the winter of 1847–48. Bell's route extended from the Madawaska River to the Muskoka, during which his crew battled snowstorms and illness, and ate a diet consisting mainly of ox meat. In his diary, he frequently mentioned the abundance of rock in the district he surveyed. Nevertheless, in his report to the commissioner of Crown lands, he wrote, "With respect to the features & character of the Country I would beg to state that from the Madawaska River [to] the Muskako [*sic*] River the country is uneven and hilly throughout, but in my opinion the chief part of it is quite fit for settlement."[9] And yet further on in his report he warned, "The greatest objection that at all exists in respect to the whole territory is the great abundance of Rocks."[10] On a more optimistic note, J. Stoughton Dennis, who also identified rocky sections, reported in 1861, "I think it will be found that the land comprised in the outlines shewn [sic] on the official maps of the Department as the Townships of Stephenson and Brunel will be for agricultural purposes much above the average quality of that of the Ottawa country generally."[11]

One would think that the harsh weather and ubiquitous rock would have led these men to question their own recommendations, and yet they likely knew that their reports were crucial to the government's decision to settle the Shield and were anxious to hand in favourable reports. And as surveyors, not agriculturalists, their knowledge of soil suitability might have been sketchy at best. For these men not only considered the harsh terrain but the proliferation of trees, which they regarded as indicative of fertile soil. Vernon B. Wadsworth described his 1860–64 surveys in a comprehensive memoir, frequently mentioning rocky land and swamps in Muskoka. However, he was generally enthusiastic about the region as suitable for settlement, and observed, "The country passed through [around Huntsville] was well timbered with pine, hemlock and hard-woods with not much rocky land and well suited for settlement."[12] However, he also opined that the district lacked the fertility of southern Ontario.

In 1975, more than a century after the Free Grants Act was passed, the Department of Agriculture commissioned a report on Ontario soil capabilities. The acreage examined did not include built-up areas in towns, provincial parks, Indian reserves, or any area used for other than agricultural purposes. The soil capabilities were classified by number. Class 1 was the best land, considered to be "suitable for production of common field crops," but as the classifications rose in number, the soil capabilities fell. Class 6 soils were considered suitable only for grazing purposes, and Class 7 soil hit rock bottom — land that was unsuitable for agriculture. Of the total of 997,120 acres of Muskoka land that the report examined, 879,681 acres were Class 7 soil, which is 88 percent.[13] Admittedly, this statistic does not include the entire Muskoka district, but it gives us an idea of how little arable land the district is considered to have. Naturally, we can forgive free grant proponents for lacking information from a government report published more than a hundred years later, but surveyor reports show that many had harboured misgivings a century before.

The most damning report probably came from James William Bridgland. In 1852, he surveyed Muskoka, and, while he found some areas of the region tillable, his 1853 apologetic report issued troubling news: "I must express my regret and disappointment, in being unable after so much labour and time expended in the exploration, to report anything concerning the lands examined, which will prove satisfactory, as to their value, or elligibility [sic].... The country northward of Black river, may be described as one vast field of granite rock.... I beg leave again, to express my regret, as to the general result of the survey."[14] John Charles Rykert had hinted that surveyors who reported negatively about the free grant lands were rarely hired a second time. Despite his discouraging report, Bridgland kept his job, as he continued to be active in the surveying of colonization roads and in 1864 became superintendent of his department.

The surveyors who set out the two-hundred-acre free grant lots followed the custom of earlier decades by shaping them into perfect rectangles; this formation would have made sense with the relatively flat land in southern Ontario, where rectangular-shaped farms would fit into the grid pattern of major roads and concession lines. In Muskoka, however, the land is rough and hilly, replete with lakes, rivers, and swamps, and, of course, rocky outcroppings. Attempting to box settlers into rectangular lots without consideration of the rough topography created a sort of lottery: some settlers could luck into a farm with a good deal of fertile land, others were stuck with rock. Had the surveyors been more flexible with the shape of the lots, the amount of fertile land a settler received could have been maximized. Admittedly, many surveyors seemed to have had little knowledge of agriculture, and shaping lots individually would have been a logistical nightmare, but it might have benefitted settlers.

Near the end of 1868, the free grant lands were subject to yet more criticism, although this time it was the government's failure to provide a solid infrastructure for the settlers that was under attack. Charles Landy MacDermott, an Englishman, travelled throughout Ontario to scout out opportunities for prospective emigrant friends back home. His subsequent pamphlet, *Facts for Emigrants: A Journey from London to the Backwoods of Canada*, was forthright when it came to the free grant district:

The man who takes a Free Grant must, if he chooses a good lot, be in the heart of the woods, — he is isolated from other settlements; — he has no road, no market, no school, no agricultural society, no post office, no mill, no church. He is living among settlers as poor as himself, and he cannot consequently hire out for wages, and whatever is done has to be done solely by the settlers themselves, without any extra assistance. Settling on a Free Grant in the townships just opened by the Government means several years' exceedingly heavy labour and much privation and hardship.[15]

MacDermott concluded that he would rather pay $100 to the Canada Company and reap the advantages it offered. Would-be emigrants must have been confused by the disparate information they were receiving: the trick would be to decide who was telling the truth — men such as MacDermott, who had nothing to gain or lose by reporting negatively on the free grants, or men such as Stephen Richards, who supposedly had everything to lose if his free grant scheme went awry.

Chapter Two

Setting the Wheels in Motion

When a person has it in view to come to Muskoka, let him as much as possible abstain from reading any of the books published on the subject.... I must say that the warmth of their colouring and the unqualified praise they bestow greatly misleads ignorant people.[1]
— Harriet Barbara King, *Letters from Muskoka by an Emigrant Lady*

On February 2, 1869, a rather florid *Globe* editorial stressed the need for "intelligent and reliable" emigration agents in Britain. "We want, for the purpose, no flashy, foolish slips of quasi-gentility, such as have too often made the officials of our Emigration Bureau a hissing and a bye-word, but shrewd, active, pushing, pleasant, intelligent men of business.... [It] will be too disgraceful if this season is also allowed to pass, and everything connected with immigration left in the same condition of helpless bemuddled confusion and indifference, which has been characteristic of all our official doings in that department for many years past." Now that the scheme was a reality, it was time to encourage settlers, many of whom would be emigrants, to make Muskoka their home. This would require a good deal of publicity both in Canada and abroad, and the Dominion and Ontario governments increased their efforts to place emigration agents in offices in Britain and Europe. In fact, Canada had been actively seeking emigrants in Britain for a number of years.

Alexander Carlisle Buchanan was appointed chief emigration agent in Canada by the British government in 1838. By the 1860s, however, he began to report to the Canadian government directly. He recommended that the government should be installing emigration agents in Britain, and, as a result, the first to be sent was Anthony B. Hawke. Born in England, he had been an agent in Canada since the early 1830s and became chief emigration agent for Upper Canada in 1835. After years working in Canada, he spent 1859 and 1860 in Great Britain travelling across the country promoting Canada as a destination for emigrants. His work was later continued by William Dixon, an Irish-born Canadian businessman who was sent to Liverpool in 1866 as an emigration agent representing Canada. After a short stint in Wolverhampton, he was transferred to London in 1869. Dixon worked in many capacities: first and foremost he was engaged in disseminating information about Canada to the British press and to British emigration agents, as well as lecturing assemblies of would-be emigrants. Judging by his rapid advancement in Britain, he must have been extremely competent. By 1872, he was overseeing other agents in Britain and Europe: Henry J. Larkin in Dublin; Charles Foy in Belfast; David Shaw in Glasgow; and Canada's continental agent, the multilingual Edward Simays, who was based in Antwerp. Dixon died in 1873, and was replaced by John Edward Jenkins, a British barrister and author.

Although politicians in both the Ontario and Dominion parliaments complained that these agents were chronically underfunded, these men certainly made good use of the resources at hand. Their offices were a repository of pamphlets, maps, rail, and steamship fare information — they even provided copies of Catharine Parr Traill's *The Female Emigrant's Guide, and Hints on Canadian Housekeeping*, published in 1854. The agents advertised the benefits of emigration to Canada in local newspapers, sent posters to public libraries, railway stations and hotels, and they travelled throughout their respective countries and regions giving lectures, displaying Canadian produce at agricultural shows, and setting up lantern slide shows in order to acquaint viewers with all that Canada had to offer the prospective settler.[2]

In a progress report dated February 24, 1870, published in the Ontario *Sessional Papers*, Thomas White, the special commissioner for emigration for Ontario, based in London, England, outlined his itinerary as he crossed Britain spreading the word about Ontario as a destination for emigrants. In the past year, he had lectured in towns and cities that included Kendal, Rochdale, Leeds, Inverness, Stirling, Newcastle, and Darlington, quite an achievement for one man. Obviously a stickler for efficiency, he reminded his superiors in one report that William Dixon, his federal government counterpart, had run out of emigration pamphlets at his office, which was an "embarrassment" to the government.

One can only hope that the government was quick to restock Dixon's supply of pamphlets, as they contained plenty of information for intending settlers, and were frequently updated. By 1869, the Ontario government had published the awkwardly titled *Emigration to Canada: the Province of Ontario: Its Soil, Climate, Resources, Institutions, Free Grant Lands, &c., &c.,* and the pamphlet was reprinted, with minor alterations, in 1871 and 1874. Inside these pamphlets were map inserts indicating Ontario's townships, followed by chapters that encompassed a whole range of topics, from geographical and population data to a description of the province's climate, manufacturing capabilities, mines and minerals, religions, laws, education, postal system, railways, canals, roads, taxation, banks, currency, and cost of living. An entire section was devoted to the free grant lands, and the 1869 issue featured a commentary about an article that had appeared in the Montreal *Daily Witness*, which had been titled "Cruelty of sending newly arrived Immigrants to worthless Free Grant Lands." A letter to the paper's editor penned by Thomas McMurray, the newspaperman who attended the Dominion House dinner in 1870, was included. Indignantly, he wrote: "The great mistake that some immigrants make is this: They settle down on inferior lots on the road, and expend their means there in preference to going back a mile or two into the bush, where they might have good soil that would sustain their families. There is an abundance of good land in the Muskoka district; only let the settler make a wise selection."[3] Why suggest in an emigration pamphlet that there might be problems in the free grant district? As negative reports were obviously not uncommon, perhaps the government deemed it best to meet them head-on. And yet the whole exercise reminds one of the carnival game of Whac-A-Mole: each time a critical report popped up, the free grant architects had to move quickly to knock it on the head.

One of the hardest-working emigration advocates was the commissioner of agriculture and public works, John Carling. Today we would be more inclined to connect him with the brewery business rather than emigration, as Carling inherited his father's London, Ontario, brewery in 1849. He was the founding member of the London Board of Trade, as well as a director of southern Ontario's Great Western Railway, but politics became an important calling for him. He eventually served, concurrently and consecutively, as a Conservative member of Parliament in both the provincial and federal governments. During the early free grant years, as Ontario's minister of agriculture and public works, he was an active proponent of the scheme. In his annual report to William Pearce Howland, the lieutenant governor, which was published in the 1871 Ontario *Sessional Papers*, he described his office's efforts in publicizing the free grant lands. Of the sixteen thousand placard advertisements of the free grants he'd had printed, fourteen thousand were sent to England and two thousand were distributed to emigration agencies and public places across the Dominion. He was especially happy to report on the success of the visit to Muskoka made by the Reverend Styleman Herring, the English vicar from Clerkenwell.

Carling went on to assure the lieutenant governor that the free grant lands were largely a success, although he requested that aid be given to some emigrants who were too poor to erect a house or purchase food before their first crop was sown. Carling suggested that the government look into building small houses in the back country of the district and clearing a few acres for settlers in distress: this could be paid back in installments in a few years. For all his enthusiasm, it is clear that Carling was already aware that the free grant scheme needed some reinforcement from the government, and that, just a few years after the scheme was initiated, there were those who were in urgent need of aid.

While the government was publicizing Canada through their emigration agencies, there were less-official efforts to recruit settlers. Probably the most diligent promoter of the free grants was Thomas McMurray. McMurray had two passions: Muskoka settlement and the temperance movement. (One wonders if he and Styleman Herring, another ardent temperance advocate, imbibed any of the ales and wines generously served during the many toasts at the Dominion House dinner!)

McMurray's early years reveal that he was a strong self-motivator who was highly driven to succeed. The son of an Irish weaver, he was born in Paisley, Scotland, in 1831. Early in his teenage years, he was elected president of the city's juvenile branch of the Total Abstinence Society, a worthy endeavour for one so young, although it could be that this rather precocious but upstanding position didn't endear him to his fellow schoolmates! McMurray was a man who constantly reinvented himself. In his early years, he worked as a weaver, and then, at age fifteen, he embarked on a short-lived career as a sailor. However, upon arriving in New York on his first voyage across the Atlantic, he decided to abandon that occupation and found work with the New York and Erie Railroad Company. He returned to Scotland in 1848 and became a salesman in Glasgow and, later, in Belfast.

One day in 1861, he chanced upon an advertisement in the Belfast papers reporting that John A. Donaldson, an emigration agent based in Toronto (and, incidentally, another member of the Dominion House gathering), would be meeting aspiring emigrants at the Plough Hotel in that city. McMurray was so impressed with the information on Muskoka provided by Donaldson that he made what seems to have been a snap decision to emigrate to Canada with his family. By this time, he had been married for ten years to Elizabeth, a second cousin. She must have been a very tolerant woman to have withstood McMurray's decision to embark on yet another adventure, or perhaps she harboured the same restlessness and looked forward to a new life in Canada. Upon arriving in the district in May 1861, he purchased four hundred acres near Bracebridge on the south bank of the Muskoka River and hired Richard Hanna, a government employee who was opening up the Peterson colonization road, to build him a house and clear ten acres. As it happened, McMurray chose well — his land was fertile. In his *Free Grant Lands* book he described the family's first night — Hanna had not yet provided a roof for his home upon their arrival, and they were soaked in an overnight deluge. By morning, however, they were able to light a fire, change into dry clothes, and begin their new adventure. McMurray had a distinct edge over many of the settlers he encouraged to settle Muskoka a few years later. Although he had to part with some capital to purchase his lot, he was wealthy enough to avoid the arduous tasks of clearing the land and building a shelter.

McMurray was an ambitious man, not one who was content to stay on the farm. He had a growing family to support — his profile in the *Dictionary of Canadian Biography* suggests he had at least nine children — and he was soon drawn to politics and the business community. By 1867, he was the first reeve of the townships of Draper, Macaulay, Stephenson, and Ryde, and on September 14, 1869, he launched the first edition of his weekly newspaper, the *Northern Advocate*, initially based in Parry Sound before it was relocated to Bracebridge within a year. McMurray claimed a print run of one thousand copies weekly, and many of these he mailed to England, Scotland, and Ireland, thus becoming an unofficial emigration agent. The *Northern Advocate*'s editor, James Boyer, who became the first clerk of the town of Bracebridge in 1875, described the *Northern Advocate* in an article in the June 8, 1905, edition of the *Muskoka Herald*: It "advocated vote by ballot, abolition of statute labor, a change in the system of expending the money on roads, a better rotation of crops in farming, etc." Not only could McMurray expound in editorials about the desirability of Muskoka for settlement, he was able to promote his own businesses while preaching temperance into the bargain. In the December 21, 1869, edition of his newspaper, he ran an advertisement for the *No. 1 Canadian Temperance Song Book*, the music "selected and arranged by Thomas McMurray." In the same issue, he posted an ad for his bookstore in Parry Sound, which also dealt in "furniture, stoves, lamps, watches, clocks, jewellery, fancy goods, Indian curiosities, books, paper." It stands to reason McMurray would encourage settlement in the district — his store needed customers, his newspaper needed subscribers, his songbook needed choristers.

McMurray was a diligent founding father of Muskoka, but he suffered somewhat from tunnel vision where Muskoka settlement was concerned. In his *Free Grant Lands*, he attacked critics with exaggerated vehemence — in other words, he protested too much. In a chapter titled "The Black Picture," he described the journey made by a delegation of eighteen to twenty farmers from the town of St. Mary's near London in southwestern Ontario. They had travelled to Muskoka sometime prior to the publication of McMurray's 1871 book (he doesn't specify the date of their visit) to see the free grant lands in person; their report appeared in the local paper, the *Vidette*. The farmers' observations were blunt: "After tedious and hopeless wanderings ... they returned indignant and disgusted at the imposition of paid agents and rascally speculators; and they declare … that the idea of its [Muskoka] being an agricultural country is a barefaced piece of imposition, invented by tricky sharks, who are fairly coining money out of the necessities of the new comers…. The soil is nearly all sand and rock…. The residents are chiefly emigrants from English cities, who know nothing of farming, and are easily victimized by the Government agents and private adventurers."[4]

McMurray was incensed by their observations, probably sensing that he could be one of those "tricky sharks" being referred to. He replied: "[We] must congratulate the Government upon the wisdom they have manifested in selecting London as the seat of the Lunatic Asylum, as we have evidence before us that at least 18 or 20 will shortly be fit subjects for admission into that great institution, and the expenses of removal will not be great."[5] Further on, McMurray suggested that these farmers had conducted their business on a Sunday, which was most unseemly, and that they "got on the spree" in Port Carling, which, considering his advocacy for the temperance movement, was even worse!

It could be, in McMurray's defense, that it was in the interest of these southern farmers to denigrate Muskoka. Fear that giving away free grants to settlers could devalue their own land may have been the impetus behind their harsh attack. Perhaps McMurray should be commended for at least including criticism of the free grants in his book, but he might have gained more credibility had he faced that criticism with a more tactful approach. That said, his guidebook — co-written with James Boyer, the town clerk — is probably the best primary source for information on early Muskoka settlement: it is a compendium of newspaper articles — mostly gleaned from his own newspaper — letters pertaining to settlement, hints for emigrants, a detailed study of each township in the Muskoka area, even some pen-and-ink illustrations and poetry that showcased Muskoka's many delights. Though McMurray may have exaggerated Muskoka as an ideal farming district, he certainly was as dedicated to the free grant scheme as were the emigration agents on the government payroll.

～

Opportunities for emigration to Canada were being considered by British emigration enthusiasts, as well. One of the most ardent free grant advocates was A. (Armine) Styleman Herring, the vicar from East End London who attended the Dominion House's banquet. Herring presided over St. Paul's, Clerkenwell, an extremely poor parish, and knew firsthand the lack of opportunities available to the hardworking but unemployed parishioners under his pastoral care. He ran his emigration society from his handsome 1760s Georgian terrace house at 45 Colebrooke Row in Islington, just steps from the Regent's Canal and several streets north of his Clerkenwell church. For some time, Herring's congregation met at a hall on Allen Street, but it finally moved into its own church in 1875, at the corner of Goswell and Pear Street.[6] Herring's was a "friendly" society, supported by subscription and the small weekly contributions of its members. The Free Grants Act came at a particularly convenient time for him. In the years prior to the passing of the Act, London was undergoing a severe financial depression, precipitated in a large part by the failure of the Overend, Gurney and Company bank on May 11, 1866, otherwise known as Black Friday. Answering the call for social reform and relief, philanthropic societies sprang up to remedy the plight of the city's poor, and Herring's Clerkenwell Emigration Society was particularly active. Herring was perhaps one of the most interesting characters in the free grant saga, yet he has remained somewhat of an elusive character. His name appeared frequently in reports on emigration, as well in regard to various other philanthropic endeavours, but the only apparent solid biographical information on him appears in a curious little book titled *Nearly Forty Years Exclusively Among the Poor of London*, published in 1896, the year of his death. There is no author recorded on the title page, although the British Library cites Herring as the author in its catalogue. The book lavishes praise on its subject, and is written in the third person, which seems an odd way to write an autobiography. While the book contains a preface by an S.C. Harford, who could be the author, it *is* possible that Herring wrote his own biography in praise of himself. This seems unlikely, though, as Herring seems to have been a fairly self-effacing man.

Born in 1831, Herring was the son of Armine Herring, the rector of the parish church in Thorpe St. Andrew, and a descendant of Thomas Herring, an Archbishop of Canterbury in the eighteenth century. The village church, on the Yarmouth Road leading into Norwich, is idyllically set, as it faces the scenic River Yare. According to *Nearly Forty Years*, Herring turned down the opportunity to carry on his father's comfortable position at Thorpe, where "he might have lived amongst his oldest and dearest relations and best friends a quiet, peaceful and easy life. Of his own accord he gave up all this, that he might ... spend his life in the service of his Master, in one of the poor, densely-populated districts of this great metropolis."[7]

Herring gained a great deal of respect throughout his career: the cover of the July 29, 1881, edition of *Hand and Heart: the Church Herald and Review* featured a portrait of a pensive-looking Herring, a handsome and extravagantly mutton-chopped man. Inside, an article about Clerkenwell described his many philanthropic achievements. On one occasion he sent financial aid and rice to India to alleviate famine, and on another, he paid the funeral expenses for bereaved parishioners whose family members had perished when an excursion boat, the *Princess Alice*, sank in the Thames in 1878, resulting in the loss of about six hundred lives. In fact, Herring went beyond mere financial aid — as he helped identify bodies from the disaster, he made an important observation. In the October 25, 1878, issue of the *Sanitary Record*, he was singled out as having connected the condition of the bodies to the condition of the water in which they drowned. Having mentioned Herring's contribution to the findings pertaining to the polluted waters of the Thames, the *Sanitary Record* then quoted him: "It is remarkable that the corpses picked up below the fatal spot were the soonest decomposed, showing undoubtedly that the London sewage, with its outfall at Beckton, has a deleterious effect." Herring subsequently donated water filters and medicines to the city. Such anecdotes suggest that Herring was a man of integrity. This trait was exemplified by his tireless emigration endeavours. Unlike other "philanthropists" who were eager to use Canada and other British colonies as a sort of dumping ground for the poor, Herring was careful to make the distinction that he was sending out hardworking, honest but unemployed emigrants.

Many emigration societies of the time didn't always make such a distinction. They were mainly in business to lighten the burden on England's Poor Law expenditures by emptying workhouses and clearing the streets of paupers. One of the first off the mark was Lady Hobart, born Mary Catherine Carr, whose East London Family Emigration Society began to send emigrants to Canada from London in 1868. Although there does not seem to be a record to indicate if any of her emigrants were sent to Muskoka, Thomas McMurray, in his *Free Grant Lands* guidebook, paired her with Herring for special commendation of her work. In 1884 she delivered a lecture to a workers' meeting at the Home of Industry in Spitalfields, chronicling her past successes transporting the city's poor, whom she claimed had been ravished by cholera, famine, and fever, to Canada. She sent eighty-four emigrants to Canada in 1868; in 1869, more than a thousand; and in 1870, another thousand. The address, titled "Help for the Helpless, London's Bitter Cry Hushed in Canada," which was later published as a pamphlet, revealed her true intentions. "Is it not possible that hundreds of those families now in destitution and want might be removed [to Canada]? Could they not be removed from a place where there is no room for them, where they are *not wanted*, where they are *in the way of each other*, and can hardly get food to eat, and know not how to earn sufficient for rent, not to speak of clothing?"[8] Her language is significant: "where they are *not wanted*" speaks for itself; the word "removed," used twice, suggests that she regarded poor prospective emigrants as mere pawns, subject to the whims of the emigration authorities. Her agenda certainly contrasted with Herring's more sensitive approach to the poor.

At about the same time as the free grant scheme was being developed in Canada, the National Emigration League, a collection of British emigration societies, frequently lobbied the government for state-aided emigration to the colonies. However, on the whole, the laissez-faire governments of the day were uninterested in becoming active in emigration. On June 3, 1869, in London, a delegation of members of the National Emigration Society made an impassioned plea for state-aided emigration to the Right Honourable Earl Granville, Britain's colonial secretary at the time. The delegation included Styleman Herring, John Edward Jenkins, and John Bate (the society's secretary and author of a guide to the free grant lands published that same year), as well as the Canadian emigration agents William Dixon and Thomas White. They left in the expectation that their plea would be addressed, but as time went by they failed to achieve their aims. On December 25, 1869, *Jackson's Oxford Journal* published Herring's letter to the editor, in which he chastised the guardians of the country's workhouses for failing to promote emigration to hard-working but impoverished inmates. He claimed that in the past year the guardians "assisted only 32 persons to emigrate!!!" This paltry number was a far cry from the thousands of emigrants Lady Hobart claimed to have sent to Canada, although perhaps the guardians used more discretion, and empathy than Lady Hobart when selecting prospective emigrants. Herring encouraged readers to donate their Christmas and New Year's gifts to the emigration cause, most especially to the Royal Canadian Emigration Society (presumably another name for his Clerkenwell Emigration Society — it changed from time to time), which he headed up.

Herring must have foreseen the difficulties he would have with the government. According to an 1871 report by William Dixon, Canada's emigration agent in Britain, Herring had originally suggested that he requisition a parcel of land in Ontario to form a colony, which would be called New Clerkenwell. The March 22, 1969, edition of the *Brisbane Courier* contained a reprint of an article from the *Standard* (presumably the London newspaper) that described Herring's intentions. He was raising funds in order to purchase a block of land in Canada that he would have parceled out in five, ten, twenty, forty, or more acres for the aspiring emigrants under his care. Although the article's author suggested that many of these skilled labourers were probably not suited for the agricultural life, he thought the plan showed some promise. However, New Clerkenwell never came about: Dixon advised Herring against such a scheme, predicting great hardship for the emigrants and doubting that a public subscription could raise sufficient funds. Once these hopes were dashed, Herring must have seen state-aided emigration as his only hope.

In 1870, when Sir Robert R. Torrens, a British Liberal MP, persuaded Prime Minister William Gladstone, a fellow Liberal, to support a motion in the House of Commons to solicit state-aided emigration, Gladstone acquiesced. On March 1, 1870, the motion was put to the vote, but it led to an overwhelming rejection, with 48 in favour, and 153 against. Considering Gladstone's majority government and his famed powers of persuasion, the outcome was surprising. Herring must have been discouraged, but he remained resolute in his efforts and continued with his emigration society, despite his belief that government support of emigration would be beneficial.

In the very early years of the free grant scheme, any doubts concerning the free grants had probably yet to reach Great Britain in any major way, and so Herring was likely unaware that there were already murmurs of discontent. On January 14, 1869, he wrote to Thomas White, the special commissioner for emigration for Ontario in Great Britain, expressing a keen interest. "By the last mail, I am informed that the Government of Ontario has determined to make a Free Grant of two hundred acres to every bona fide settler. This will be an *"immense boon"* to the working classes of Great Britain about to emigrate to Canada.... We have in St. Paul's, Clerkenwell, London, carried on with *great success*, a society based on the sound principles of *self-help* and *mutual-help*."[9] Herring added, "The year 1867, especially in the winter, was most woefully felt by the working classes of Britain. The piercing song uttered by dozens of fine stalwart men as they walked from street to street singing, 'We are poor working men, and have got no work to do' had a most powerful effect upon the hearers." Herring had already published advertisements in British papers for his Canadian Emigration Association (another new name!). A short notice in the *Pall Mall Gazette* on January 5, 1869, informed readers that the society was helping "a select body of poor but most deserving men residing in Clerkenwell and Central London" to emigrate to Canada. Among the five subscribers listed at the bottom, Herring topped the £10 donation of "C.S." with one of £10 10s. In his letter to Thomas White, he plugged his own little pamphlet, *Emigration for Poor Folks*, which he was selling at the bargain basement price of one pence (two if it was mailed). In the book's dedication to the Lord Mayor of London, Herring explained, "My spiritual duties as Minister in a very large and poor London district will I hope be deemed a sufficient excuse for the imperfections of my frail attempt, in this little book, to benefit my poorer brethren."[10]

Emigration for Poor Folks offered advice on fundraising for emigration, suggestions on setting up emigration clubs, and information on wages and the cost of food and clothing in the colonies. Herring also included rates for sea passages, and finished up with homely advice — among them packing tips and admonitions concerning sobriety and godliness. Most significantly, he rather astutely warned readers to "[b]eware of land sharks and proprietors of dismal swamps in unheard-of places. Working men don't generally buy pigs in pokes."[11] Unaware of the irony at this early time, he then made a special endorsement for Muskoka. "Free grants. This is the best country for a poor man." Of course, he couldn't have known then that the region that had caught his attention was home to many "dismal swamps in unheard-of places." Herring's and White's correspondence was included in the Ontario *Sessional Papers* of 1869. White seemed heart-ened by Herring's intention to send hard-working emigrants to Canada, rather than paupers. In January 1869 he wrote: "It is gratifying, however, in this connection to be able to state that the idea of relieving distress by sending to the colonies the inmates of the Poor Houses, forms no part of the present policy of these committees. The determined stand taken by all colonies against what is known as 'pauper emigration,' has had the effect of preventing any attempt to force it upon them."[12]

Herring was a staunch self-help advocate — in fact, his emigration society's motto was "To help those who help themselves." When settlers ran into trouble, he was quick to point out that they had either been intemperate or were not helping themselves, and therefore were respon-sible for their own misfortunes. The self-help philosophy was a popular Victorian concept famously espoused by the Scottish reformer Samuel Smiles. Self-help was widely advocated as a means for the poor to rise above their circumstances in order to achieve success — philanthrop-ists in particular were willing to help the poor, but only if they were seen to be deserving of help and contributed in some way toward their own success. But it could be argued that Herring and other self-help adherents had misinterpreted Samuel Smiles's philosophy. In his book, titled *Self-Help*, Smiles included numerous platitudes about the benefits of self-help, yet he also observed, "But the man who is always hovering on the verge of want is in a state not far removed from that of slavery ... and in adverse times he must look either to alms or the poor's [*sic*] rates. If work fails him altogether, he has not the means of moving to another field of employment; he is fixed to his parish like a limpet to its rock, and can neither migrate nor emigrate."[13] Even Smiles knew that if a person's circumstances were really dire, self-help wouldn't be sufficient to lift him from poverty, and that the state or a sympathetic philanthropist may have to come to his rescue.

∼

While these efforts were underway to raise the profile of the free grants both in England and in Canada, some less-than-desirable publicity sur-faced in England. Joseph Nelson was an Englishman who had been engaged in public works projects in both Canada and the United States over a thirty-year period. In 1869 he wrote a letter to the Right Honourable G.J. (George Joachim) Goschen, president of the Poor Law Board in London, which was a comprehensive report on the desirability of emigration to both the United States and Canada. With reference to the district north of the settled parts of Toronto, between the Ottawa River and Georgian Bay (presumably the free grant district), he was adamantly opposed to settlement. "These lands are intersected by a large amount of rock, lake, and swamp; the climate is severe, and unfit for any but the hardiest agricultural settlers and lumbermen…. The question may be asked, [i]s there any portion of the Dominion of Canada capable of absorbing the great mass of the surplus population of the mother country now out of employment?" Answering his own question, he concluded, "In the present state of the Dominion and its trade relations with the United States, there is not."[14] As with the National Emigration League members, he felt the government should take a more formalized approach to emigration and proposed the formation of a British and North American Emigration Company, which would be established on "commercial principles," rather than the current models that simply strove to rid Britain of the pauper population.

Not only were the free grants under some scrutiny, but the aims and abilities of philanthropic emigration societies such as Herring's were also being questioned as early as 1869. John Edward Jenkins, the successor of emigration agent William Dixon, was one of these critics. Jenkins wore many hats: he was a barrister, a politician, a social reformer, and an author. Curiously, his satirical novel *Ginx's Baby*, published in 1873, portrayed an open-air preacher said to have been based on Styleman Herring, who was one of the most notable open-air preachers in London.[15] And yet, despite honouring Herring in his novel, Jenkins did not mince words when describing the philanthropic work of such emigration enthusiasts. In an 1869 pamphlet titled *State Emigration: An Essay*, he wrote: "Charitable Emigration can never be extensive enough to afford the requisite relief. The funds required for the removal of hundreds of thousands, the organisation, discipline, facilities, and conveniences of transport, the guarantee of good conduct and repayment of monies advanced could only be secured with Government resources and authority."[16] He also warned that the colonies were complaining that England was sending out paupers, merely to be rid of them in the mother country. In a strong plea for state involvement in emigration, Jenkins was direct: "Moreover I urge that [e]migration ought not to be regarded as a scheme for a philanthropist, it should be the policy of statesmen — not as a work of charity, but as the business of Government."[17] Herring would probably have agreed with Jenkins's sentiments, as he, too, had canvassed for further state involvement in emigration schemes, although the wholesale dismissal of his philanthropic efforts might have stung a bit. But Jenkins's sentiments are certainly not without merit — organizing emigration on a grand scale would take a great deal more resources than philanthropists such as Herring could possibly access.

∾

As the second year of the free grant scheme was coming to a close, disturbing stories were emerging from the backwoods, as well. In part five of a feature article in the *Globe*, titled "A Trip Through Muskoka and Parry Sound," published on September 22, 1869, the author initially presented a cheery, humorous portrait of Muskoka life, describing contented settlers and peaceful Indians (although the author was outraged that Indian men lolled about in their canoes while the women did the paddling). But as the article progressed, it seemed that all was not well in Muskoka. The writer confided that many settlers had fled the district, overcome by the lonely wilderness and poor farming prospects. Settlers complained to the author that roads were not being built across fertile tracts but instead on "rocky ridges," which meant the most inviting parts of the country were inapproachable. The settlers suspected that Richards had a "grand financial scheme.... They suspect that once the most sterile tracts have been opened up, the free-grant system will be dropped and the fertile tracts *sold* for cash." There is no evidence to prove these settlers were justified in their suspicions, but it does indicate that Richards had failed to gain the settlers' trust. The article added that there was a "want of elasticity in the free grant system." If a settler's land proved to be unfit for cultivation, he was stuck on it — "no more free grants for him." As a result, "many good emigrants [were] forced through sheer starvation to go elsewhere," which is something many settlers could ill afford. Finally, he complained that squatters from the days prior to the passing of the Free Grants Act were told to leave even if they had already cleared their land. Unless they paid out fifty cents per acre immediately, they were out of luck.

The article concluded, "For there was not one of the Company but was deeply impressed with the fact that the whole policy of the Government toward the district is narrow and vicious and obstructive in the highest degree." This was quite a turnaround for the *Globe*, as previously it had cautiously endorsed the scheme. It must have been difficult for new settlers to decide what the truth actually was — should they believe the government, which was actively endorsing the free grants, or articles in the press that condemned them? Considering that by this time settlers were streaming into Muskoka claiming their free grant of land, they must have decided that the government, elected by the people, had their best interests at heart, and would not offer land that could not sustain them as farmers.

Chapter Three

The Long Trek to Muskoka

Send them out;
Send them out;
To the South and to the North!
With our love and with our prayers
Let our Emigrants go forth!
It is not that we love them not.
It is we love them well;
We cannot bear to see them here
In want and suff'ring dwell. [1]
— Styleman Herring, *Emigration to the British Colonies*

News of the free grant scheme spread rapidly, largely as a result of the emigration agents' publicity efforts both in Canada and Britain. Before long, emigrants were preparing for a new life in Muskoka. The free grants also attracted emigrants from across Europe — Germans and Scandinavians, in particular — and from the United States, but Canadian emigration authorities chose Great Britain as the main conduit for new settlers, anticipating that citizens from the mother country would most easily fit into Canadian society. In June 1869, Thomas White delivered a lecture in Liverpool and urged his audience (which included a "sprinkling of ladies") to emigrate to Canada, because "in going there you remain as you are to-day — British subjects, subjects of the same great empire, and owing allegiance to the same great, glorious, and gracious Sovereign."[2] White's audience seemed highly receptive to his lecture; he was met with prolonged applause, good-natured laughter, and cheers. White employed an earnest and compelling approach with his prospective emigrants, showing them a good deal of respect by using his powers of persuasion rather than simply bullying the audience into emigrating to Canada. As we have seen, emigration enthusiasts such as Lady Hobart were not always so circumspect. Unlike emigration agents, she was in the business of compelling rather than persuading, and it would seem that reluctant emigrants had little choice in the matter. If one's circumstances were desperate, refusing aid to emigrate would be out of the question. Such a dramatic move across the ocean would take serious contemplation, and yet there was often little time for a prospective emigrant to ponder over the pros and cons of such a move. Lady Hobart's East London Family Emigration Society was said to have given as little as three weeks for families to prepare for their crossing of the Atlantic. Such a drastic move is difficult to contemplate — for those eager to leave Britain, perhaps a speedy departure was desirable. But for those who dreaded leaving their homes behind, the very prospect must have been intolerable.

No doubt emigrants had various reasons for leaving Britain for Canada — not just poverty. In the case of the free grants, the adventure of settling in a country as new — and as wild — as Canada would suit younger emigrants who might have found the strictures of a class-structured, conventional society such as Britain stifling. No doubt there were nefarious reasons to emigrate as well: debtors or criminals on the run might enjoy the anonymity of life abroad. Family feuds might drive others to leave home. Younger sons of the gentry who didn't stand to inherit the family farm would be interested, as would tenant farmers who longed to farm their own land, rather than a landowner's. Whatever the emigrants' circumstances, such an enormous undertaking would have a lasting impact on their lives. One can imagine the mixed feelings and heartache for those who said farewell to family and friends, knowing in all likelihood they would never meet again.

The first decision for those emigrants who could choose their time of departure was when to arrive in Canada, and for that decision they received contradictory advice. Some emigration advisers, such as

Thomas White, suggested autumn was a good season to emigrate. His reasoning was that a settler could build his house before winter set in, then hire himself out to a lumber company or begin to clear his own land during the winter months. This was fine and well, except he would have to have sufficient capital to get him through the winter if work wasn't available. Also, lumber camps tended to frown upon commuting, which, of course, would be difficult in the bush, and it seems safe to assume his wife may not have been thrilled to spend the winter alone in her little shanty in the bush, possibly with children, while her husband was miles away felling trees. On the other hand, Thomas McMurray suggested the beginning of May was the ideal time to settle Muskoka. He predicted it would take one week to locate a lot, and one more to erect a house. Then all the settler had to do was clear some land and sow some crops, which would soon provide the family with sustenance. McMurray had quite a knack for making pioneering look like a walk in the park, but his time frame seems more reasonable than White's. Such contrary information must have confused would-be settlers. It is most likely, however, that emigrants simply sailed when the opportunity arose and took their chances on the timing of their voyage.

Another consideration would be capital: how much money was required to emigrate to Canada? Calculations on this amount varied widely, depending on the point of view of the one advising on the subject. Those eager to attract settlers were more likely to gauge that a small amount of capital was needed: why discourage an emigrant even before he or she arrived? Styleman Herring estimated that about £20 to £50 would be sufficient, but this would be a hefty amount for those who earned only a small wage or who were unemployed. Even if they could borrow or raise that amount, it seems hopelessly unrealistic for settlement. The *District of Muskoka Settler's Guide*, published by the District of Muskoka Settlers' Association (its president was A.P. Cockburn) in 1868, advised that £100, or $500, would be required to properly set up a farm, although, in an effort not to discourage would-be settlers, the author added that hard-working farmers might manage on much less. And yet two years later, Thomas L. Hanson, an English clergyman living in Woodbridge, Ontario, just northwest of Toronto, wrote a letter to the London *Times* on February 12, 1870, that contradicted the adequacy of that more generous amount.

In a scathing indictment of the free grant scheme and of the emigration clubs that sent people to Canada, he wrote: "Men of means, with, say, some $4,000 or $5,000 capital — these may, after a long and hard battle with the forest, succeed; but mere labourers coming here will have to struggle with much hardship, suffering and loss."

One settler's guide, *The Undeveloped Lands in Northern & Western Ontario*, published in 1878 under the "sanction of the Commissioner of Crown Lands," made a handy assessment on how a budget of $250 (£50) could be stretched. It listed the necessary items a settler would need, along with a breakdown of the prices of each. Among those items were flour, pork, potatoes, tea, herring, and salt; seeds; farm tools; kitchen implements; bedding; and livestock (one cow and one pig). Handily, the tally was $247.40, leaving the settler with $2.60 to splash out on.[3] As with other guides, *The Undeveloped Lands* made sure that the cost of setting up a viable farm neatly tallied with the amount of capital it suggested was needed. Surprisingly, this calculation didn't take into consideration the cost of passage, which would presumably have to come out of this budget.

Capital would diminish as the costs of passage were taken into consideration. Many of the emigrants boarded Allan Line ships for their voyage to Canada. A sample of one of the line's posters was published in Styleman Herring's 1871 *Letters from Abroad* emigrant guide. The cost of a steerage ticket from Liverpool or Glasgow to Quebec City was six guineas (one guinea was worth a pound plus a shilling). The price included "a plentiful supply of Cooked Provisions," and the baggage transfer cost from ship to train was waived. Upon their arrival in Quebec, emigrants were escorted by emigration agents onto the Grand Trunk Railway cars without charge as they made their way to Toronto. However, a Northern Railway advertisement included at the back of Thomas McMurray's 1871 *Free Grant Lands of Canada* indicated that passage to Bracebridge from Toronto (via train, stage wagon, and steamer) cost $3.75, with no mention of baggage fees. Joseph Dale was an Englishman who wrote *Canadian Land Grants in 1874*, with the intention of correcting misinformation about the free grants made by most guides. Despite his awareness that he would come under attack for his observations, he was determined that emigrants not be misled. Contrary to the information on the Northern Railway's poster, he suggested that emigrants could expect a free passage to Muskoka, but warned of onerous baggage charges. As well, there were further costs on the requisite steamers and stage wagons that were required after the railway met the terminus at Severn Bridge.

Having raised or borrowed money for the trek across the ocean, emigrants would have to decide what to pack for the long journey ahead. Wealthier emigrants would probably bring as much as possible — furniture and housewares would certainly make their new home familiar and cosy. But for the poor, only the bare necessities would be possible. Herring suggested that emigrants should only take what was necessary on their voyage, while conceding that small ornaments could be packed — to alleviate homesickness. Feather beds and warm clothing were top of the list, and a "ship kit" was a necessity: a coarse sacking bed; a blanket or rug; a one-gallon water can; knife, fork, and spoon; tin basin for soup; hook-pot; tin plate and wash basin; and marine soap. Thomas McMurray suggested that little possessions brought from home could be a comfort to those arriving in a new land. He also advised emigrants to take "some fresh eggs packed in salt, a piece of smoked ham, a few pounds of cheese, some pickles; and, if you are Scotch, a quantity of oatmeal cake."[4] Presumably McMurray was offering his advice to steerage passengers only, to supplement the ship's offerings — you can bet travellers such as Herring or Charles Marshall dined more heartily during their voyages. Passengers fortunate enough to have avoided the privations of travelling in steerage accommodations had a much more comfortable existence. A menu dated May 6, 1875, for the dining room on the Allan Line's *Prussian* steamship listed the breakfast bill-of-fare, presumably for cabin passengers: spatchcock (a butterflied chicken) and mushrooms, fried ham and eggs, potatoes, mutton chops, dry hash, Yarmouth bloaters, fried tripe and onions, devilled kidneys, beef steak and onions, and, finally, porridge (presumably provided for the Scots on board!).[5]

~

Having amassed what capital they could and said their goodbyes, emigrants now faced the prospect of a transatlantic voyage, an adventure very few had probably experienced. The early sailing ships could take up to five weeks to cross the Atlantic; by the 1870s, the ocean crossing by steamship could be a relatively short ten days. As the journey was now quicker, the provisions for passengers improved: fruits, vegetables, and fresh meat remained unspoiled for the duration. While the extreme discomfort suffered by steerage passengers is the stuff of legend, some emigration enthusiasts downplayed the poor conditions for those below deck. Lady Hobart, herself making a crossing in 1868 to Canada, slipped downstairs to check out the emigrants' quarters and rather facetiously claimed, "I have myself gone into the steerage at all hours of the day, and have found the people contented and exceedingly well looked after."[6] How unfortunate that she didn't record how her visit was received by the steerage passengers, who, unlike her, had not been fortified that morning by a ten-course breakfast, such as was served on the *Prussian* a few years later. Her friendly visit just might have raised a few eyebrows from less affluent voyagers. Fierce Atlantic storms, seasickness, inferior food, close proximity to fellow voyagers, the filth resulting from overcrowding, and the trepidation of crossing the ocean to a new country could hardly have eased the minds of those emigrants who sailed "below" Lady Hobart.

In his *Letters from Abroad*, Styleman Herring published a correspondence sent to him by a passenger whom he had accompanied on his visit to Canada aboard the *Peruvian* in August 1870. Herring explained that "Mary Lucy H." taught school in London, Ontario, and her husband was employed in the city as a carpenter. Her letter gives us an insight into what proved to be a rather harrowing journey. She described her family's arrival in Liverpool at four in the morning on August 4, presumably having started out from London. At the quayside, each family was presented with beds, cans, plates, knives, and forks. They then waited for a steam tug to take them to the "splendid" *Peruvian* steamship, which Mary Lucy described as 400 feet long (it was actually 312 feet), with 116 crew and a total of 700 on board. They were treated to a breakfast of hot rolls and butter, and at first the journey promised to be quite comfortable. But the disagreeable state of steerage soon became apparent. The *Peruvian* set sail on Thursday, August 5, and arrived in Quebec on the fifteenth. Mary Lucy described her experience in a letter to Herring:

> [Aug. 5?] We had a kind Christian Captain, and Mr. Herring was very kind…. I did not like the look of my

sleeping place when I got in; I could not sleep at all; it was like a small box, and some sleep above you; dreadful hot, could scarcely breathe....

[Aug. 6] Weather rather rough, the ship rocking very much; sickness very bad; such a scene you never did see.... John very sick.

[Aug. 7] Baby and I have not been sick yet; lovely morning; service in the first cabin, a lovely place, seats covered with red velvet. The captain read the prayers, Mr. Herring, the sermon.... We had service in the cabin again in the evening, afterwards some beautiful hymns on deck; one of them was, "Shall we meet beyond the river?" My thoughts went back to the old friends at home, and I felt very sad.

[Aug. 8] The sea is getting very rough, obliged to take in the sails; towards evening it became worse; it was very cold, snowed quite fast, and the waves swept everything away that was loose on deck into the sea.

[Aug. 9] Much worse; no one could stand on deck; down below we had to hold by a rope to keep from injuring ourselves; several were hurt; baby and I were dashed from side to side; I was screaming, "O my baby." [The sailors] … had hot fowls and beautiful pies of all kinds for their dinner; they often gave me some, and they often came on deck and sang with us. We had generally fresh beef, potatoes and soup for dinner; Friday [was] soup and fish, because there were many Irish Catholics on board; we had as much as we liked to eat.[7]

On August 11, land was sighted at Newfoundland, where it was bitterly cold, but Mary Lucy admired the icebergs and "small whales" in the water. When they finally arrived in Lévis, a small village across the St.

Lawrence River from Quebec City, on August 15, they were temporarily housed in emigration sheds. Eventually, they were loaded onto railway cars for the trek to Toronto. This journey took three days and two nights, and was a miserable, noisy affair: the passengers were not even able to change clothes. Upon arrival in Toronto, Mary Lucy and her family were served dinner in an emigration shed, then they changed trains for the city of London, in the southwestern region of Ontario. London was an established, go-ahead community in the 1870s — innovations such as gas street lighting had been in place since the mid-1850s — and the family soon settled in. They rented a house for four shillings a week, and John was employed almost immediately. And yet, as successful as her emigration experience seemed to have been, Mary Lucy was already homesick. "If some parts of earth and sea are so lovely, what must heaven be; it makes one long to be there, where we shall not have to part with those we love, but shall meet never to part again."[8]

As we can see from Mary Lucy's destination, not all of Herring's emigrants went to the free grant lands. In fact, it's difficult to decipher what percentage of his emigrants eventually made their way to Muskoka — certainly the free grant lands were his main focus — but it is also apparent that many made their homes in southern Ontario. In an article published in the January 1, 1874, issue of the British periodical *After Work*, Herring gave a breakdown of where emigrants were sent on one "hypothetical" voyage. Muskoka topped the list with 750 settlers; individually, the other destinations received fewer, but collectively they absorbed many more: Chatham became home to 680 emigrants; London, 622; Collingwood, 600; and Hamilton, 541.[9] It is probably fair to conclude that emigrants with some capital, education, or skills were more likely to settle in the older parts of Ontario, where land was fertile and towns built up: those who settled the free grant lands likely lacked the resources of their fellow emigrants.

∾

For those less fortunate than Mary Lucy — who merely had to change trains in Toronto to get to her destination — the journey north to Muskoka would not have been an easy one. And yet, in his guidebook to the free grants, Thomas McMurray made the journey sound simple. "Muskoka is conveniently situated, being only 121 miles distant from the

City of Toronto.... The geographical position of the settlement is good, forming as it does almost a bee-line of travel from Liverpool to Victoria."[10] The words *conveniently* and *bee-line* were a little disingenuous, considering that the distance between the two cities is 7,373 kilometres! More to the point, Toronto is a "convenient" 5,447 kilometres from Liverpool. Not only is that still a very long distance, we must remember that it is unlikely that many of these emigrants had strayed far from their own neighbourhoods in their lifetimes. After their long journey by ship and train to Toronto, the real hardships began with the journey north.

This trek was aptly described by Harriet Barbara King, a British officer's widow. In 1871, she left her home in Calais, France, to join her youngest son, who had sent glowing reports of his free grant in Muskoka. With the Franco-Prussian War virtually being waged at her doorstep, King, her daughter, and son-in-law, a professor at a local English language school, were joined by her eldest son, who was disenchanted with his office job in London. Already in her early sixties, she found the journey arduous. In her memoir (which may have been slightly fictionalized), *Letters from Muskoka by an Emigrant Lady*, published in 1878, she described her experience. She suffered from violent seasickness during the passage to Canada — and unlike Mary Lucy, she enjoyed the relative luxury of a cabin, not steerage. After landing in Quebec, King boarded a train for Montreal, then changed trains for Toronto. Once there, she and her family stayed in the Rossin House, a rambling but grand hotel at the corner of King and York Streets. Mrs. King wasn't happy with her lodgings, frequently getting lost in its vast corridors; she confessed she was "most *supremely uncomfortable*" that night. She found the staff rude, and seemed to have missed the dinner hour, which was a shame, as an 1869 menu from the Rossin House Hotel featured no end of delicacies, from boiled, roasted, and cold meats, soup, curries, and vegetables, to pastries and desserts.[11]

The following afternoon, she boarded the train from Toronto to reach Belle Ewart on the west side of Lake Simcoe, embarked on a steamer to Orillia, then changed to a "filthy, over-crowded little boat"[12] for the trip to Washago. From there she proceeded by stage wagon for Gravenhurst, arriving after dark. "The road was most dreadful — our first acquaintance with 'corduroy' roads."[13] From Gravenhurst, where Mrs. King had spent the night in a local hotel, she took a steamer to Bracebridge and while there consulted with the commissioner of Crown lands to sign for her lot. Then came a fifteen-mile wagon ride through the forest to the small village of Utterson, and finally, at the end of the day, after the horses were refreshed, they travelled an additional six miles to arrive at her son's log home, located near Lancelot, a tiny, isolated hamlet about eight miles (as the crow flies) west of Huntsville in Stephenson Township. Mrs. King lamented the loneliness of her surroundings. It's safe to conclude that when she arrived in Lancelot, it must have seemed the end of the earth.

Despite Mrs. King's complaints about her long journey to Lancelot, a fledgling transportation infrastructure had been set into place prior to the passing of the Free Grants Act. As early as 1859, location tickets were being distributed for the Muskoka Road, which at the time was in the early stages of construction. The road finally reached the vicinity of Huntsville in 1863. However, in those early years it was extremely rough, as it was cut through rocky outcrops, swamps, and over hilly land; in fact, it could barely be called a "road" by any but the most avid Muskoka promoters. Thomas McMurray certainly fell into this category. He wrote glowingly of Muskoka's road network: "While we cannot boast of having advanced so far as to have much macadamized road, still we are highly favored beyond many settlers of former days."[14] McMurray's definition of *much* remains vague, but tempting his readers with visions of paved byways in Muskoka seems to have been a mite misleading. The Parry Sound Road was begun in 1861; stretching from the Muskoka Road west to Georgian Bay, it was completed in 1867. Eventually branching off the Parry Sound Road were the Rosseau, Nipissing, and Northern Roads. Despite their rough condition, they did at least provide access, however limited, to the free grant lands.

When roads and bridges showed early deterioration, the township began to rely on statute labour as a solution. This practice became a bone of contention, for many settlers had their hands full already maintaining their own farms, without having to repair and build roads they considered the government's responsibility. Naturally, it was a cheap way for often cash-strapped municipalities to achieve an infrastructure of roads throughout the whole province, requiring only a pathmaster to supervise and enforce settlers' obligations. In Muskoka, it was an arduous task, with farmers supplying their own tools and implements in order to carve out roads on the rough terrain of the district. Statute labour drew much criticism — in fact, James Boyer, the editor of the *Northern Advocate* and Bracebridge town clerk, went so far as to identify statute labour as "that relic of a barbarous age."[15] Farmers could bargain with the pathmaster: those with some capital could hire others to do the work or lend a team of horses in exchange for their own labour.

The condition of the roads throughout Muskoka was a constant source of discord: the government blamed the settlers, who were often too occupied with farming, for not contributing to their upkeep; the settlers in turn blamed the lumber companies for damaging roads with their heavy loads; and naturally, everybody blamed the government for not doing their part to keep the roads passable. In summer, those built in swampy areas would become mired in mud, and bridges were often burned out from forest fires or simply gave way under frequent use. Winter brought some relief as snow and ice at least provided a hard surface. Whatever the season, many roads were crudely planned, with abrupt drops and steep ascents. Such harrowing byways made quite an impression on author Charles Marshall: "From Washago on Lake Couchiching to Gravenhurst the route passes for fourteen miles through a singularly picturesque tract of savage scenery. Precipitous broken hills, crowned with dense pine and beech, rise on every side; abrupt masses of granite block the way. The ragged road-track plunges violently down the hill-slopes to the corduroy bridge over a stream at the bottom, and toils painfully up the opposite slope."[16]

The prospect of a rail system throughout Muskoka was another incentive to settlement that was slow to materialize, but must have encouraged settlers. By 1853, the Ontario, Simcoe and Huron Union Railroad Company (renamed the Northern Railway a few years later) joined Toronto north to Aurora, and by 1855 stretched all the way to Collingwood on the shore of Georgian Bay. In 1867, a spur line led to Barrie. With the passing of the Free Grants Act in 1868, it was acknowledged that rail transport would enhance settlement opportunities, as well as being of benefit to the lumber companies, and so, in 1869, the Toronto, Simcoe and Muskoka Junction Railway Company was founded. Travelling by rail would be a decided improvement for settlers, considering the uncomfortable conditions of the roads at the time. The railway reached Orillia in 1872, Washago in 1873, Severn Bridge in 1874, and Gravenhurst in 1875. However, the railway didn't reach the heart of Muskoka until a decade later: Bracebridge was linked up in 1885, and finally, the following year, the line was hooked up, via Huntsville, to the east-west CPR line at North Bay.

There was much fanfare when the train arrived in Gravenhurst in 1875, with more than 250 dignitaries aboard, many of them representatives of the Northern Railway Company. The Orillia *Times* reported: "On the arrival of the train at the Company's dock, where the steamers were waiting their arrival, a regular steam greeting took place, by the locomotives and steamers whistling without cessation for about five minutes, the brass band on the *Nipissing* playing an appropriate air."[17] One longs to have been a witness to such an ear-splitting and joyous event. It reveals just how important decent transportation was to a new, isolated settlement such as Muskoka. Rail transport facilitated later settlement, and certainly was a boon to the tourist industry, which was still in its early stages, but, as with the colonization roads, the early settlers in Muskoka had many years to wait until they enjoyed its benefits.

In contrast to the difficulties and slow construction of road and rail transportation, Muskoka's extensive waterways provided a comfortable means of travel, and were utilized from the beginning of settlement. Although Mrs. King didn't enjoy the jaunt on her "filthy, over-crowded little boat," the journey must have been superior to the bone-jarring ride over corduroy roads. Recognizing a need to develop water transport in Muskoka, A.P. Cockburn, the local businessman and politician who attended the Dominion House celebrations and one of the members of the Legislature who contributed to the debates on free grants, was one of Muskoka's greatest advocates, and he, along with Parry Sound entrepreneur William Beatty, was said to have convinced John Sandfield Macdonald that the free grant scheme was viable. In 1867, he founded the Muskoka District Settlers' Association in Orillia, which was set up to help early settlers become established and to dispel misinformation about the district. Cockburn opened a general store in Gravenhurst, but his vision for the district surpassed mere shopkeeping. Showing considerable insight, he realized that transportation throughout the Muskoka lakes was crucial both for settlement and for the anticipated tourist industry. He initiated his Muskoka Lakes Navigation Company with its first steamer, the *Wenonah*, in 1866, which plied the waters of

Lake Muskoka, and by 1869, he had launched the *Waubamik*, which serviced Lake Rosseau. By 1871, the *Nipissing* was added to the fleet, and sailed between Lake Muskoka and Lake Rosseau via the new locks at Port Carling. The company's *Segwun*, built in 1887, is still moored in Gravenhurst. To this day, the steamship plies the lakes of Muskoka, its whistle a haunting sound on summer evenings.

In the Huntsville area, water navigation was slower to be developed. Beginning in 1877, Captain Alfred Denton's *Northern*, a side-wheeler steamer, navigated lakes Mary, Vernon, and Fairy, linking Port Sydney on Mary Lake to Huntsville. He later expanded his fleet, but came into competition with Captain George Marsh, who had his own steamers on Lake of Bays. When Denton intruded onto Marsh's territory on Lake of Bays, Marsh retaliated, basing some of his fleet on the waterways that Denton had previously presided over. The two became fiercely competitive, and in 1895 Marsh took over Denton's business, founding the Huntsville and Lake of Bays Transportation Company ("Transportation" was later changed to "Navigation"), which catered to settlers, lumbermen, and tourists alike.

It is not surprising that the Muskoka lakes were such a draw for the tourist industry. Early visitors were entranced by these scenic waterways. John Clay, a Scotsman, journeyed to North America in 1874 to scout out emigration opportunities for Scottish settlers. He rhapsodized over the beauty of Muskoka lakes and rivers. "Embarking on board the neat steamer *Nipissing*, she steams away from the wharf up the Lake of Muskoka, a picturesque sheet of water, studded with rocky islands of all shapes and sizes, wooded to the water's edge with pine and cedar trees. It was evening, and the scene was exquisite.... It is a romantic sail up that stream, and brings to mind many a story of Indian warfare and trapper life...."[18] Perhaps Clay got a little carried away here with his image of bellicose Indians, but he does provide a pleasing image of early water transportation.

Whatever means settlers used to reach their Muskoka destination — rail, road, or waterway — as they traversed the free grant lands, they must have taken heart at the beauty of the region they had chosen as their new home. However, beautiful scenery would not sustain them — they had to hope that the rugged landscape would provide them with a decent living.

A.P. Cockburn's Wenonah, *the paddle steamer that transported Styleman Herring and Charles Marshall to Bracebridge on September 14, 1870.*

A view of the rapidly growing town of Bracebridge circa 1873.

Thomas McMurray's pen-and-ink portrait opposite the title page of his Free Grant Lands of Canada *guide*.

Styleman Herring's calling card. It appears that Herring had corrected the date, for the alteration of Jan. 7, 1877, is clearly an addition. If the date is accurate, this photo would have been taken between Herring's two trips to Canada. Ian Denning of London, England, found the card in the pages of an early history of Clerkenwell.

Stephen Richards, Ontario's first commissioner of Crown lands and the driving force behind the free grant scheme.

Premier John Sandfield Macdonald, whose Liberal-Conservative coalition endorsed the free grant scheme from the first debates in 1868.

A poster sent out to prospective British emigrants, signed by John Carling, commissioner of agriculture and public works for Ontario. Thomas McMurray printed this poster in the back pages of his Free Grant Lands of Canada.

MPPs in Ontario's first Legislature in 1867, casually posing for the camera. John Sandfield Macdonald can be seen behind the top hat on the table, centre front.

Chapter Four

The Pioneering Life

Come to the land of rivers,
And groves of goodly pine —
A land to last forever,
To be both yours and mine;
Our rulers now, God bless them,
In wisdom they designed
Free grants of land to give away
In this most favoured clime.[1]
— "The Backwoodsman's Song,"
sung to the tune of "Auld Lang Syne"

The raw beauty of the Muskoka landscape certainly enthralled the first visitors from Britain, a country whose ancient forests had long disappeared. Many saw a pure, unspoiled environment where settlers could live off the land in a rural setting, unsullied by the growing slums and unpleasant dirt and noise of machinery common in Britain's factory towns. Canadian emigration adherents continually emphasized the country's natural beauty, and made it clear that Canada should be regarded as an agrarian country first and foremost. In fact, their advice to new emigrants was to leave cities such as Toronto immediately upon arrival, as there was no end to temptations — from taverns to brothels — that could lure them away from the gentler and safer countryside.

Many towns and cities across Ontario by the 1870s were already hives of industry, but the image Canadian emigration officials wanted to project was of a country that would remain primarily rural, with its rustic wilderness always on the horizon. The free grant lands fit this image well: settlers would be living a clean life, safe from the corruptive influences of the big cities, in houses literally fashioned from the forest surrounding them. And yet sprinkled across this rural idyll were Muskoka's fledgling towns, which soon became small hubs of commercial enterprise and cultural pursuits.

At the time of the Dominion House banquet in 1870, Bracebridge was by no means an unimportant backwater. Thomas McMurray, in his 1871 guide, listed businesses that included hotels, Crown land and registry offices, general stores, blacksmith shops, a drug store, bookstores, bakers and butchers, and carpentry shops. Recreational activities flourished: a regatta was held in October of that year, and the community enjoyed public concerts and lectures. An annual fall fair had been instituted, which attests that there were some settlers enjoying the fruits of their labours, and local agricultural societies were formed throughout the district. James Boyer was pleased when, in the early 1870s, Muskoka took second prize for spring wheat at the agricultural fair in Toronto, and he himself won second prize for his plums and grapes. It is evident that those with good land were becoming as successful as the businessmen in Bracebridge and in the district's other town centres.

And so this was the thriving town that greeted the "celebrities" who had gathered at the Dominion House in September 1870, and it is likely that Styleman Herring and Charles Marshall were impressed by the busy little community in the backwoods. But their Canadian hosts — politicians, businessmen, and emigration agents — were not representative of the poorer settlers who found themselves struggling to carve out a farm in the wilderness. Many of the men in the delegation, if not most, were, at least by now, far removed from the rigours of actual settlement. If we are to believe Charles Marshall's account of the day following the past evening's revelries, their visit seemed to be about the *novelty* of settlement. Having sampled the hotel's wines and ales till two in the morning, the government dignitaries and their guests might have had heavy heads the next day, but that didn't stop them from enjoying a sort of *Boy's Own* adventure in the backwoods. They were about to have an opportunity to play pioneer.

Daylight on September 15, 1870, revealed to Marshall and his fellow Muskoka visitors a pleasing aspect of Bracebridge. Marshall described the log huts, wooden cottages, and two- to three-storey frame houses that were set at various elevations on the hilly ground, rising from the torrent of the waterfall below. He enthused about this "romantic" setting, where sawmills were in full operation and the shops were bustling and prosperous. After a sightseeing tour of Bracebridge, the official party began their travels, stopping for a swim in Lakes Rosseau and Joseph, and fishing from canoes and rowboats supplied by nearby settlers. Finally, that evening, they set up camp where a team of workmen was cutting a channel to merge the two lakes. In the spirit of the previous night's party, the merry band of government representatives and their guests set up a "magnificent fire of pine logs" next to their canvas tents and sat down to a hearty dinner of broiled fish and pork, washed down with "cooked" tea. Joined by some backwoodsmen and the canal workers nearby, they sang songs — "patriotic, sentimental and comic," according to Marshall. Finally, long after the stars appeared, one by one they disappeared into their tents and wrapped themselves in blankets, no doubt weary from the day's activities. The only disturbance to their slumber was a "wild cry of alarm" emitting from John Sandfield Macdonald's tent — obviously unused to campfires, the premier had dreamt he was "in a house in flames."

The following morning, the men nailed a plank of wood to a nearby pine tree, and Marshall suggested they name the campsite in honour of the premier. "In the name of Her Majesty Queen Victoria and of the Dominion of Canada, the Reverend Mr. Herring christened the place Port Sandfield."[2] During their forays throughout the backwoods that day, they happened to meet up with a group of Herring's London parishioners who had settled in the district, and Marshall recorded that they were delighted to see the face of an old friend. These settlers were all satisfied with their new lives, he was happy to report. But one cannot help but wonder if this was a chance meeting. Herring and Marshall would hardly wander through the bush at will — they had to be guided by those familiar with the terrain. Most likely those guides would have been Thomas McMurray and A.P. Cockburn, men desperate to put the free grant lands in a good light. It would hardly have done for Herring to meet up with *dis*satisfied settlers from his old parish of St. Paul's, Clerkenwell, considering the risk of having Marshall record their complaints. Admittedly, Herring and Marshall *could* easily have met up with successful farmers. But it is their universally positive experience that leads one to be slightly skeptical.

The day's activities included a little lesson in wood-chopping, and although Marshall found himself to be useless at the task, Macdonald was pronounced "an old hand." In his detailed recording of the day's events, Marshall explained how a log cabin was constructed, going so far as to speculate that in three or four years a new squared timber house might be built, a type of architecture that could become "a model type for a gentleman's country residence."[3] With his land cleared and quaint log house built, Marshall suggested the farm would look like a piece of Old England. After about five more years of prosperity, there was almost no limit to the farmhouse's potential. "If [the settler's] tastes are pretentious, he decides on a stone residence, with a handsome portico. But, more probably, he will build an elegant frame house, with pretty balconies and a wide verandah."[4] This description almost exactly describes Thomas McMurray's handsome house, the Grove, the home he had built after he moved to Bracebridge from Parry Sound in 1870. A three-storey gabled frame house encircled by a two-tiered wraparound verandah, the Grove would have exemplified the heights of success that Marshall seemed to believe were in the reach of every settler.

This is not to criticize Marshall for his unbridled enthusiasm, but his account has the whiff of British gentility about it. We can assume that the closest he had come to pioneering was his campsite dinner, and even that was likely prepared by his hosts. And needless to say, a balmy September night in Muskoka is a stark contrast to one in January. The snug little log cabins he described would be bone-chilling in winter — and pork, fish, and tea were not always in abundance as they were that evening. Marshall was in the company of like-minded free grant enthusiasts; he simply didn't ponder the hardships that these allegedly contented settlers might undergo in real life. During this well-orchestrated jaunt, Marshall and Herring were likely flattered by the attention they received from their high-ranking hosts, and they naively accepted their hospitality and didn't seem to question the uniformly rosy picture that had been created just for them. Most important, the misinformation that Marshall and Herring took back with them to England meant that many emigrants would be ill prepared for a life in the bush.

~

Settlers who arrived in the free grants district from older parts of Canada — southern Ontario, in particular — would at least be familiar with Canadian agricultural methods, the cold winters, and relatively short growing season. But British emigrants with agricultural experience would have found a very different experience in Canada, especially in Muskoka. Although they would relish the prospect of owning two hundred acres free of charge, these farmers were used to a softer climate and a longer growing season. As well, Britain's vast forests had been cleared for centuries and its fields cultivated with tried-and-true crops that had weathered the course of time. Now these new emigrants had to familiarize themselves with new types of crops suitable for a colder climate and a more rugged terrain.

So many aspects of the settlers' lives would be altered. For example, in Britain, farmhouses were often centuries old, or rebuilt with a ready supply of materials available from the local village or town; now the emigrants would be dwelling in crude log cabins of their own making. Back in Britain, produce that couldn't be grown on the farm, as well as household necessities, could be purchased from nearby shops. Settlers living near towns could avail themselves of these items easily, but those on isolated farms would not be so fortunate. The low population density in Muskoka's backwoods would be a shock, as well. Much of the British countryside is sprinkled with small villages, many of which are in sight of one another. Most have their own ancient inn with public house attached, a row of small shops, a church, and a village school. For entertainment, there was an established country calendar of traditional social events. Although nineteenth-century industrialism saw an exodus from the countryside to Britain's major cities, extended family would often live nearby, and an established social network would be in place. Gradually, such a network was woven into the fabric of Muskoka society; but in the early years, emigrants from Britain's rural areas must have longed for the centuries-old rhythm of country life in their homeland. Lastly, the dark, impenetrable Muskoka bush was home to predators, which had long been eradicated in England. In Canada, the existence of animals such as bears, coyotes, wolves, and lynx would not only endanger livestock left out in the open, they'd probably frighten the living daylights out of anyone who encountered them.

A far greater adjustment would be required of urban emigrants, especially the parishioners from St. Paul's, Clerkenwell. While many were living in legendary Dickensian poverty — disease-ridden, filthy, overcrowded dwellings — we must remember that nineteenth-century London was a hugely advanced society compared to the backwoods. Too often "pioneer" histories are presented in a sort of vacuum, as if kerosene lamps and horse and buggies were the last word in mechanical innovation. But emigrants who had arrived from London had enjoyed a fairly sophisticated city. London was thoroughly modern by nineteenth-century standards — by the 1860s, for example, the metropolis boasted gas-lit streets and a steam-powered underground transportation system. As well, London was then, as it is now, a city of living history, something that was severely lacking in Muskoka. In place of London's groomed public parks, ancient churches, and handsome Georgian residential neighbourhoods were endless bush and forest, log and frame shanties, and basic shops and public buildings. And despite popular depictions of Victorian urban depravity, London streets were lively at all times of the day, with entertainers, food purveyors, public houses, and penny theatres providing distractions for all but the poorest. Most significant, the camaraderie of the streets, where neighbours chatted across front stoops and over backyard garden walls, even in poorer districts, would be a part of everyday London life, enabling a social cohesiveness that emigration to a rough, isolated region would irreparably shatter.

∽

After all the tribulations settlers had undergone to reach their free grant lot, the moment they set eyes on their chosen land must have been an emotional one. They had put a great deal of trust in the emigration agents and their pamphlets, the philanthropists who had helped them arrive in Canada, and in the land agent who helped them locate their lot. Now they stood before their plot deep in the Muskoka bush, perhaps near neighbours, perhaps intensely isolated. To call them brave hardly does those settlers justice, for their destiny was to be decided by the fertility of the land that stretched before their eyes. For those who had chosen a fertile, rock-free tract, visions of a prosperous farm would validate the decision to settle Muskoka. But others must have felt an instant panic as they regarded a rock-strewn, hilly terrain, knowing immediately that it was not likely to be arable by any stretch of the imagination. Exhausted from their journey north, the unluckier settlers must have wondered what on earth they had gotten themselves into.

A settler who had left his family in emigrant accommodation or at a hotel in the nearest town would at least have a few days to hobble together some sort of shelter before his wife and children joined him, but there must have been others who brought their families directly to their lot, especially if they were in the more remote regions of Muskoka. It would have been essential, before all other tasks, to build a shelter for the family. Unlike Thomas McMurray, many settlers couldn't afford to pay someone to do this task, and a good many of them likely lacked basic carpentry skills. Housing "bees" might bring out neighbours to help, but these jolly events (as they are usually portrayed) were probably difficult to organize in more isolated spots. That said, as any visitor to a pioneer village can attest, the structure of the first log home was basic to the extreme, lacking the quaint rusticity that Charles Marshall described. Harriet Barbara King, having left her comfortable mansion in Calais, was not too pleased with her log accommodation. "The house inside was simply one tolerable-sized room.... It was built of rough, unhewn logs, chinks of wood between the logs, and the interstices filled up with moss. There were two small windows, and a door in the front. The size of the house, eighteen feet by twenty-five."[5] In the centre of the room stood a "hideously prominent and ugly" stove, as well as pots, pans, and kettles. As their furniture had not arrived, they made use of boxes and a chest for sitting down to meals. King longed for her French-manufactured bedding, vastly superior to Canadian-made linens, she confided.

Not everyone found a log cabin as repugnant as Mrs. King, however. *The Ontario Farmer*, a periodical published out of Toronto, was far more enthusiastic. In its April 1869 issue, an article titled "Roughing It in the Bush" suggested that such a dwelling could be the epitome of rustic beauty.

"A well-built log-house is by no means to be despised. There is a fitness about it that cannot fail to impress every observant mind. The wonder is that with the architectural capabilities possessed by the new settler, better and more permanent log-houses are not erected. Below we give an illustration showing how a little skillful exercise of taste will make a log-building attractive and ornamental."[6] Presumably, Mrs. King's son, who had built her house, lacked any "architectural capabilities." If he'd had such talents, he might have built a home that resembled the one illustrated in *The Ontario Farmer*: a pretty little log cottage with a central gable and a rustic verandah fashioned from rough logs. The article gave step-by-step instructions on how to build a log home. Good-sized windows should be cut out, the roof neatly shingled, and the floor covered in planks. Allowing for the fact that not all settlers possessed the skills for building, it was suggested that "an exchange of work with some skillful neighbor" would ensure the building was soundly constructed. The whole exercise sounded so simple that it begs the question — was the article written by an editor sitting in his *Ontario Farmer* Toronto office miles away from the bush, thumbing his way through old pioneer guides offering how-to advice? This takes us back to the cynicism of "Poor Settler," the *Globe* correspondent who correctly guessed that Stephen Richards was probably some lawyer in Toronto who had never even been to Muskoka. Whenever the pioneering life was made to seem easy, and romantic, a little skepticism seemed to be in order.

Once some sort of shelter was constructed, the settler faced the real work of pioneering — clearing the land and sowing his crops. Although the more enthusiastic of emigration adherents made clearing the land seem like a relatively simple task, providing the settler was a hard worker and abstained from liquor, the process was anything but. In *The Undeveloped Lands of Northern and Western Ontario*, the authors suggested that "[t]he chopping and clearing of land is hard and at times dirty work; but it is also pleasant, and is attended by an interest, and a satisfaction, of which people never seem to tire. The axe is a pleasant tool to use."[7]

Despite such reassurances, after several hours of pleasant chopping, settlers would undoubtedly have found the clearing of even a few acres to be rather arduous. Those who could not afford to hire help with the clearing not only were obliged to take on the gargantuan job themselves, they frequently had to do so without the benefit of proper tools or livestock to aid in the hauling of tree stumps and logs. Even if a settler could afford implements, his problems weren't over. Joseph Dale, the English writer who had warned emigrants about baggage charges on the railway, asked, "How is [the farmer] to get [the cattle, horse, mule or other animal] through such a swampy country without breaking their legs, or getting them mired? So few and far are the spots where sufficient grass can be obtained, and so quickly is anything like fodder snapped up in such a country, that the whole of the emigrant's time with the labour of his cattle would be consumed in getting sufficient fodder. To log by hand is impossible, besides being too slow for any practical purpose, and so the land remains encumbered."[8]

Jane Tritton Gurney, a minister's wife from England, travelled to the Anglican Diocese of Algoma, which included the Muskoka district, and published her experiences in an article in the autumn 1887 issue of the *Cheltenham Ladies' College Magazine*. She didn't reveal exactly when she visited Canada, but it would have to have been during the free grant years. She was a keen observer of the day-to-day lives of free grant settlers, especially when describing the back-breaking task of clearing the land when implements or animals were scarce or nonexistent: "Many of the settlers come out with very little money, and they have to undergo great hardships in making for themselves a home in the trackless forest. Each tree has to be cut down, chopped into lengths, and burnt; and then it is perhaps years before the root remaining in the ground can be extracted, to allow the free use of the plough."[9]

Frederick de la Fosse was just eighteen years of age when he arrived in Canada from England. He published his memoir, *English Bloods*, in 1930 under the pseudonym Roger Vardon. Orphaned at a young age, de la Fosse was raised by relatives until he came of age and his future had to be decided. After an undistinguished school career, the family decided to send him to Muskoka to attend a small agricultural school run by a Captain Charles Grenville Harston,[10] who had settled on a lot on Buck Lake. De la Fosse had the enthusiasm and energy that land clearance demanded, but to him it was clearly still a daunting process. "The first [step] is underbrushing, that is, cutting down the small growth in the woods; the second, chopping down the heavy trees; the third, the burning off of the fallow in the spring; and the fourth, the task of rolling up the logs into big piles and burning them. As soon as this has been done, the land is ready for the first crop."[11] Tuition at Captain Harston's small "school" was £100 per year; however, Harston hardly seemed the ideal teacher. Fosse was amazed that his mentor lacked the simple knowledge that he must provide shelter for his cattle during a harsh Muskoka winter, and when de la Fosse arrived at Harston's farm he was dismayed at its condition. "To call the place a 'clearing' is somewhat of a misnomer. There *was* a clearing, certainly, of about three acres, but it was strewn with blackened logs and burnt branches. Where there were no logs, large boulders were the chief visible features. There was no arable land at all."[12]

Once the land had been partly cleared, crops had to be sown, and, as emigrants frequently arrived in summer or autumn, there wouldn't be much of a growing season left before winter set in. Without adequate farming implements, many of them would have had to resort to primitive means for planting their seeds. A telling description of this process came from Thomas Osborne, who wrote his memoirs in 1934. Osborne, who was born in England in 1859, had emigrated with his parents and siblings to Philadelphia in the mid-1860s, but his father moved the family to the free grant district in 1875. Initially, Osborne's father, William, left his wife and children in Toronto while he travelled north to purchase a squatter's lot in North Portage, just east of Huntsville on Peninsula Lake. In a short time, he summoned Thomas, who was fifteen, and his younger brother Arthur, thirteen, to join him. After making their way from Toronto by train, steamer, and stage wagon, they finally reached Utterson. From there, the two young boys trekked up the lonely Muskoka Road, finally meeting their father in the dead of night at Cann's Hotel in Huntsville.

A few days after they arrived, William taught his sons how to plant their first crop. "[Our father] gave us about a peck of cranberry beans and two sticks about eight inches long and pointed at the end. He told us to make holes about eight inches apart wherever we could among the stones, roots and stumps in a plot of cleared land at the back of the cabin."[13] Ploughing by means of a sharpened stick seems ludicrous, yet such advice was common for settlers with few farming implements. In their *Undeveloped Lands in Northern & Western Ontario*, the authors gave this rather dubious advice:

"Putting in the first crop is a very simple operation. Ploughing is at once impracticable and unnecessary. The land is light and rich. All it needs is a little scratching on the surface to cover the seed."[14] At least they suggested using a "drag or harrow" to do the "scratching," rather than the simple stick approach practised by the Osborne boys.

~

Building shelter for their families and animals, clearing an acre or two, and sowing a few seeds was only the beginning of the settlers' problems. What awaited them was a long, cold winter, the likes of which many of the British-born emigrants had never experienced. In May 1872, Edward A. White, emigration agent to the United Kingdom, reported to Archibald McKellar, the chief commissioner of agriculture, "One of the greatest bugbears which prevents persons from coming to Canada is the frightful stories told about the rigours of our winters. You can hardly mention Canada but there is a shiver and a significant remark about our cold, which convinces you at once that the impression prevails at home that mercury is down to 25° below zero nearly the whole winter."[15] Many settlement advocates boasted of the healthful qualities of a Muskoka winter; indeed, Canada's cold but dry winters are often regarded as healthier than the moderate but damp ones common in Great Britain. However, White overlooked the fact that settlers' shanties would be inadequately heated and primitively constructed, providing little comfort in cold weather. The emigrant without adequate capital would be unable to purchase sufficient supplies — blankets, heavy coats, warm footwear, for example — to see the family through the cold season.

Thomas Osborne's family found the cold unbearable. "And so we lived through the winter. I have wondered that Pop didn't lose his mind because of all the privations. As Mother had contracted inflammatory rheumatism in her hands, her finger joints swelled up very badly and were very painful. Then, too, Kate [a sister who suffered from emotional instability possibly brought on by a high fever] would have her bad spells, which, with the cold and insufficient food, were great worries to us all, especially Pop."[16] Eventually, Osborne ordered his mother and younger siblings (with the exception of Arthur) to return to Philadelphia, fearing their health would be endangered by the harsh conditions.

Of course, there were some advantages to the winter season. Tobogganing and ice skating were inexpensive pastimes, and those who could afford it would enjoy sleigh rides across frozen roads and lakes. Transportation was easier in some ways — the frozen surfaces of roads that were mired in mud during rainy seasons became easier to traverse. And as winter was the season for logging, many settlers would have had the opportunity to earn some much-needed cash.

~

Coupled with the harsh winters was the shortage of nourishing food throughout those frigid months. Many settlers were isolated from villages and unable to obtain provisions, and money was often short. If the past season's crops reaped insufficient food for winter storage, hunger remained a huge problem. King reported that her family almost starved during their first winter, living on hard salt pork, potatoes, oatmeal, molasses, rice, and flour. In 1874, the year before she left Muskoka, the family's wheat was "winter-killed," and that Christmas she described a festive dinner of "two very small salt herrings" and a "huge vegetable marrow," which she supplemented with well-buttered mashed potatoes.[17] After years spent living in the north of France, such a diet must have been tedious for her in the extreme. And her inability to source the fresh dairy, produce, and meat products she probably enjoyed in her French neighbourhood would be extremely frustrating.

And yet for some, the novelty of such a diet seemed to appeal. One of Styleman Herring's emigrants who had settled in Muskoka (or "Maskoka," as the settler identified it) had taken up 600 acres of "splendid land on the borders of Lake St. Mary." His anonymous contributor reported, "I am perfectly satisfied with my new life.... I work very hard in chopping, am already a man and a half to what I was before I left.... The country is most healthy and fertile, and will well repay the adventurers for a few years' hard work. We live on bread, molasses, and salt pork, with tea, every meal."[18] Despite the assurances of the good life in "Maskoka," one has to be a little wary of the letter's providence. Herring published several emigrants' letters in his *Letters from Abroad* and *Emigration for Poor Folks*; this was the only one from Muskoka, the rest mostly having been sent from cities and towns in southern Ontario. Also confusing is the fact that there is no Lake St. Mary in Muskoka, unless the settler meant Mary Lake. And it is one of the few letters that was not signed with either a name or initials. But despite these doubts of the letter's authenticity, there is the final irony. As with King, this settler was consuming a diet that lacked fresh meat, dairy, or produce, rather an odd phenomenon for a farmer.

Emigration guides suggested that game was plentiful in the bush and would be a handy supplement to the settlers' winter diets. It might have been a relief to British settlers that there were no poaching laws in Muskoka, but their relief would probably be short-lived. Settlers' accounts were almost unanimous as they described the dearth of wildlife and the difficulty in hunting the few animals they came across. Mrs. King had assumed that there would be a constant parade of partridges, ducks, and deer passing by her door each day, but it was not to be. Farming the land would be a full-time job, and hunting was a time-consuming endeavour that would take the settler away from his land for any number of hours or days.

Of course, more prosperous settlers on good land would be likely to have had better access to food, whether home-grown or purchased in the neighbourhood. W.E. Hamilton, a newspaper editor and emigration agent who travelled to Canada from his home in Ireland, stayed the winter of 1874–85 with a George Kelcey in the Parry Sound area, a settler whose land, according to Hamilton, was fertile clay-loam soil. He was astonished to find that Kelcey's diet did not consist solely of beans with the infrequent addition of pork, but ran the gamut of "Prime beef from throughbred [sic] cattle, delicious venison, chicken and turkey of the best, home cured hams, all vegetables which could be grown in the country and stand cellarage, with excellent tea, cream and eggs."[19] Hamilton had chosen a lot nearby but it was rocky, and his farm did not prosper. However, his description of Kelcey's frequent repasts demonstrates how the quality of a settler's farm could determine the very quality of his life.

∼

Social interactions in the bush drastically altered the lives of settlers. For example, there was the very new experience of co-existing with the Native population, especially in the early years, before they were marginalized in reserves. In some ways, Canadian settlers had a better relationship with Aboriginal people than did their counterparts in the United States and Australia. As early as the seventeenth century, employees of the Hudson's Bay Company relied on the Aboriginal population, who acted as guides, supplied animal pelts, and advised them on how to survive in the bush. Despite the inevitable conflict between the two factions, there were notable alliances and friendships as well. Two of the most often mentioned Native chiefs in Muskoka histories were William Yellowhead and John Bigwin. Yellowhead, who was Objibwa, had close relationships with the settlers and government officials such as Thomas McMurray, who, in his *Free Grant Lands* guide, confided that he had once invited Yellowhead to stay overnight in his home.

Yellowhead's Aboriginal name, Musquakie, has been said to have been the origin of the name Muskoka. John Bigwin, a Chippewa band member whose family summered on Bigwin Island in Lake of Bays, was a highly respected Native leader who had frequent dealings with the settlers, and who spent years defending hunting and fishing rights. Both of these men were said to have been centenarians (although Yellowhead's burial record in Orillia recorded him to have died at 95, Thomas McMurray claimed he reached the age of 106), quite an achievement in those days.

Commentary regarding the local Native population swung from contempt to grudging respect. In an 1858 Special Commission report, the unnamed author was openly contemptuous: "They [the Sandy Island band] have hitherto resisted all the attempts made to civilize them, and cling with uncountable tenacity to the foolish superstitions imbibed from their fathers."[20] Yet not every visitor to the district held the Native population in such open disregard. Settlers' accounts often mentioned the pleasant sight of "Indian" canoes passing by, and their delight in purchasing their handicrafts. Surveyor Vernon Wadsworth visited Port Carling in the early 1860s and seemed quite intrigued: "The Indian Village of Obogawanung, now Port Carling, consisted of some 20 log huts, beautifully situated on the Indian River and Silver Lake with a good deal of cleared land about it used as garden plots, and the Indians grew potatoes, Indian corn, and other vegetable products. They had no domestic animals but dogs and no boats but numerous birch bark canoes."[21] During his journey to North America in 1874, Scottish writer John Clay also visited Port Carling, and his observations reflected the more positive attitudes towards the "Indians" that Wadsworth had expressed:

> Those Redskins are a mysterious people, and difficult to understand; but they were civil and kind, and, through an interpreter, we had a long harangue with some of the tribe. In their way they are big gentlemen, and love an idle life. Here they dwell in peace. The Canadian Indian is not such a noble-looking man as those who inhabit the prairie, but they enjoy peace and justice. The Dominion Government have [sic] tried to preserve the race, while their neighbour's policy has been to extirpate and demoralise their red brethren.[22]

The rather idyllic Native settlements described by Wadsworth and Clay, however, were soon to become extinct — eroded first by settlement and later by tourism. As the white population settled in the area, claiming their free grants and drawing tourists to the area, most of the Aboriginal people gradually relocated to reserves on the Christian Islands, the Gibson River area, Parry Island, Beausoleil Island, and Rama. Despite Clay's admiration for the government's dealings with the Aboriginal population, over the following years governments reneged on many agreements, forcing Native leaders to repeatedly remind authorities of broken promises.

Coexisting with the Native population was not the only new experience for settlers — Harriet Barbara King described her encounter with Jake, probably one of the few Black citizens in Muskoka. When King's sons found Jake by the roadside, clearly ailing, they decided to build him a small shanty for shelter, then fed him and nursed him back to health. King noted that he was shunned by the neighbours — likely because of his race — but she enjoyed conversing with him, finding him quite intelligent. Her sons offered to pay him to clear the ground around his shanty. Sadly, the association was broken when Jake's friend Mary, a white woman, showed up with their five children, and it became apparent that they were living in sin. The Kings gave notice to Jake, sending him and Mary on their way with provisions and two dollars. Amusingly, King, unlike her neighbours, was not so bothered by Jake's race; it was his loose morals that upset her!

Mixing with those not of one's station was another new experience for many. This distinction was an early conundrum for settlers in Canada. Class distinctions were almost an institution in Britain and other European countries, where one rarely socialized with those of a lower class. Harriet Barbara King, who, as we have seen, showed compassion to her Black neighbour, was less approving of a settler who had been a ploughboy in Kent, England. "It seemed so strange to me at first, to be shaking hands and sitting at table familiarly with one of a class so different from my own; but this was my first initiation into the free-and-easy intercourse of all classes in this country, where the standing proverb is, 'Jack is as good as his master!'"[23] In time, King seemed to value her friendship with the former ploughboy, and it is to her credit that she was able to reach across the class divide to befriend him.

The daily grind of homesteading, coupled with the loneliness in the bush, must have worn many settlers down. One memoirist, Mrs. Edward Copleston, arrived in Canada from England in 1856, to settle near Orillia, just south of the Muskoka district. Although neither the date nor location quite coincides with the free grant scheme of 1868, her experience would have been similar to the settlers' who arrived north just a few years later. Accompanied by her husband, Scottish nanny, and two young daughters, she was truly daunted when she contemplated life in the woods. "I was horror-struck at the proposal of making this our future home. I could afford to admire the noble forest at a distance, but when the possibility of my being imprisoned in its vast depths for the remainder of my life was mooted, I shrank from such an ordeal."[24] Incidentally, not only did Mrs. Copleston dread living in the bush, she was monumentally ill equipped to meet the challenge. Lacking any culinary skills, she was dependent on her nanny and a helper who she rather unpleasantly referred to — at least by today's standards — as a "bush girl." She admitted in dismay that her household skills were basically nonexistent. "Unhappily, it was really too true that these very simple matters were as unknown as Greek to me, and my two bright handmaidens were equally ignorant, or feigned to be so."[25] Realizing the ludicrousness of arriving in the bush with no domestic knowledge, she added, "I could not help being both amused and ashamed of my own incapability." English middle-class girls like herself, she observed, were well versed in playing piano, singing, riding, dancing, and reading, but could scarcely bake a decent cake or loaf of bread.

During the winter months, when many men looked for work in the lumber camps, the wives and children were left alone in their little log homes in the wilderness. James Boyer was especially sympathetic toward the women, whom he suggested "had not only had their household duties and children to attend to, but who amid their struggles and self-denial of those early pioneer days often assisted the men in the rough and heavy work of clearing and planting the land, and thus assisted in laying the foundation of, and made possible, the civilization so generally and almost unconsciously enjoyed by the present generation."[26] What fears and privations they experienced can only be imagined. For many women, the simple boredom of life in the woods was another tribulation. Although Mrs. King was more capable in the kitchen than Mrs. Copleston, and had her daily tasks to keep her busy, she was unable to deal with the repetitive nature of daily life. "Had a bear jumped in at the window, or the house taken fire, a hurricane blown down the farm buildings, we should have been tempted to rejoice and to hail the excitement a boon."[27]

While depictions of pioneer life are often quite benign, especially for those who were prospering, life on the frontier had its dark side, as well. With few magistrates or constables to keep the peace, public drunkenness and crime were no strangers to the bush. Virtually every commentator on emigration or the free grants warned about the evils of alcohol. W.E. Hamilton, himself reportedly no stranger to the bottle, wrote, "Drunkenness, too, which clings like an evil spirit to the Anglosaxon race, whether under palms or icebergs, plentifully sprinkled Muskoka with moral and physical wrecks."[28] And yet, for those living in quiet desperation, a convivial drink at a local tavern would have been a temptation difficult to resist. If one could moderate their alcohol intake, in fact, a little conviviality at the local watering hole would certainly be cheering. One commentator on life in the backwoods, William F. Munroe, compared such inns to the institution of the British pub. "The tavern in Canada, especially in the backwoods, still bears something of its old English signification — it is a place of hospitable entertainment for man and beast, and, as such, is one of the prime necessities of a new country." On a cold winter night, "the sight of a roaring fire, with a glass of 'hot stuff,' [was] an almost indispensable condition of travelling."[29]

Those who were troubled in their new home would have derived some comfort from their religion. But for many emigrants, the spiritual comfort of attending regular church services was elusive; the major towns could boast a few churches of various denominations, but more remote areas precluded attendance. Travelling preachers frequently visited the district, which must have provided some solace. Most poignant was the story of a "rough farmer" whom Jane Tritton Gurney encountered deep in the bush. He hadn't been able to attend church in seven years due to his isolated location. Gurney related that "when a service was started, and the grand old *Te Deum* was sung, it was too much for him, and he quite broke down."[30]

~

Despite these poignant stories, there were, of course, settlers who were pleased with their land and their new life in Canada. Sarah Ann Spencer, who with her husband, Abel, arrived in Muskoka's Macaulay Township near Bracebridge in 1869 from the Midlands district in England, obviously was much better placed than many of her fellow emigrants. At first, they worked as tenant farmers, then took up their own free grant shortly after. In her letters home, she urged her family to join them in Canada. On August 16, 1869, she wrote, "I am doing very well again and not working near so hard. I sit down with the family and eat the best of food. It is not like that in England." By June 1870, they had moved to their own land. "[We] have a nice log house up 18 by 20. We have a new stove with all the useable articles to it such as pots and pans for which we had to give 24 dollars for.... It is really the cottage of content."[31] Her husband seemed to be absent, working on railway and road projects, but that didn't dim her enthusiasm. Evidently, their land was fertile, for she reported that they had successfully grown bushels of potatoes, swedes, turnips, cabbages, and Indian corn, and eventually they built a small mill on the property. For Sarah Ann Spencer and her husband, the free grant scheme was heaven-sent, and their success reveals how essential it was for a settler to locate on arable land.

Chapter Five

A Hornet's Nest of Dissent

It has been said that on this North American continent we like "a big thing," and certes this free grant article is big enough — the biggest, most heartless, and most decided imposition practiced on Englishmen.[1]

— Muskoka settler's letter to Arthur Clayden, 1873

While Muskoka settlers were becoming accustomed to their new home in the bush, the free grants continued to be a source of acrimony both in Canada and abroad. Debates continued in the Legislature; pamphlets were published criticizing the scheme; and editorials as well as letters to the editor in newspapers on both sides of the Atlantic weighed in on free grant settlement and, by extension, emigration. From 1870 onward, there was a steady escalation of accusations and blame. Presumably, the proponents of emigration must have been troubled by these early warnings. And yet, Stephen Richards, who was central to the drafting of the scheme, hadn't even bothered to visit Muskoka until two years after the Free Grants Act was passed. It took the same time for Styleman Herring, the vicar from East End London, to visit Muskoka, but he had a much more daunting journey than Richards. Although transatlantic voyages were not unusual in those days, it was still remarkable that Herring would abandon his parish duties for a few months in order to check up on the emigrants he had already sent over to Canada.

It could be that early criticism of the free grant scheme had already caught his attention and he began to doubt his initial enthusiasm. In the letter to the *Times* quoted in chapter three, Thomas L. Hanson, the clergyman from Woodbridge, Ontario, not only complained that Canada-bound emigrants needed thousands of pounds for successful settlement; he also disparaged emigration clubs themselves. On February 5, 1870, Hanson wrote: "Very false notions prevail at home about the prosperity of this country.… Surely these 'clubs' should pause before they send out so many here, only to encounter bitter, biting poverty." Herring was obviously incensed. On February 14, in a letter to the *Times*, he addressed Hanson's accusations with a blunt assertion: "I never heard of people starving in Canada." Herring wasn't the only person to question Hanson's account. Later that year, in July 1870, Thomas White warned John Carling that Hanson was a troublemaker, who had "calculated … to work a great deal of mischief to Canada. Indeed, I found in my travels through Great Britain afterwards, that the opponents of emigration to Canada had taken the greatest pains to circulate the letters of this clergyman, and evidently relied upon them to deter people from coming to this country."[2] Such letters must have troubled Herring, who not only must have been concerned by such reports, but also must have been frustrated by the fact that his continued attempts to secure state aid for emigrants were refused time and again. In March 1870, he led a delegation of two hundred members of the Cow-cross Emigration Mission Club (Cow-cross Street is in Clerkenwell) to a meeting with the Holborn Union, an East London workhouse. The members of the emigration club pointed out that the British and Colonial Emigration Society, a charitable association presided over by the Lord Mayor of London, had promised to pay half the cost of sending emigrants to Canada, and requested further funds from the board of guardians. Their request was refused. Herring was putting an enormous effort into the Clerkenwell Emigration Society; perhaps these repeated setbacks drove him to take direct action, as he was soon to visit the free grant lands himself.

The final straw for Herring, though, may have been a pamphlet titled *What Emigration Really Is*, published anonymously in London, England, in 1870 by "a resident of Canada and Australia." It could quite easily have fallen into Herring's hands, and he would not have been pleased with the author's observations. "For I find that there is great ignorance displayed on [emigration], and even those who essay to inform others, not having themselves actually gone through the experience, lead them astray to a great extent.... True, we hear accounts, and we read letters from those who have gone, giving the most glowing accounts of the places, where *they* are doing well; but do we hear nothing of numbers of others that are there and *not* doing well?" The author added, "This [free grant land] is not the *best* land in Canada, nor is it in the best part, and yet there is but slight difference, as the Government is anxious to get the wilder parts of the country inhabited."[3]

And so it was that on August 3, 1870, Herring set out from Euston station in London, headed for Liverpool, from which he would sail with 179 emigrants from his Clerkenwell Emigration Society to see Canada for himself. As we will recall from the account of Mary Lucy H., who was one of those emigrants, they boarded the *Peruvian* on August 5 and arrived in Canada on August 15. Once in Canada, Herring immediately set himself an exhausting itinerary — he claimed to have travelled six thousand miles during his journey: he visited Montreal, Ottawa, Peterborough, Lindsay, Oshawa, Guelph, Hamilton, Brantford, London, Toronto, and, as we have seen, Bracebridge. On August 27, the *Globe* gave him a warm welcome, wishing him the best in his emigration endeavours and distinguishing him as "among the first in England to publicly direct attention to Canada as a suitable field for emigration." No doubt the first few weeks of Herring's visit were heartening, as southern Ontario was becoming a prosperous region. He may, however, have already been harbouring doubts about the free grants even before he travelled north to Muskoka. At a Temperance Hall meeting in Toronto on September 10, Herring cautioned his audience of about two hundred people that perhaps emigrants shouldn't venture into the backwoods immediately upon arrival, but find agricultural work on settled farms in order to get used to the customs of Canada. This was a slight deviation from his former thinking — in the early years of the scheme, before 1870, Herring seemed to think emigrants should be able to take possession of their free grant immediately upon arrival in their new country. He claimed that all who were "sober and diligent" would succeed. He urged his audience to attend church, and to form societies with other newcomers to avoid despondency and homesickness. Lastly, he magnanimously offered to take messages and parcels back with him to England for family members. This was just one of several meetings across Ontario — if he made such a gesture everywhere he went, one can imagine that he carried home a good deal more luggage than he had brought.

Just hours before he set off for Muskoka, Herring took it upon himself to gently admonish John Carling on Canada's failings in the emigration business. Herring wrote the letter on September 13, from the Toronto address of 126 Adelaide Street.[4] Herring encouraged Carling to create emigration clubs across the Dominion, and suggested that the government should give financial aid to emigrants upon arrival. "Australia and New Zealand are now outbidding Canada for emigrants," he cautioned. Carling replied on September 20, mildly rebuking Herring. He pointed out that he was already sending out emigration circulars to Ontario municipalities advertising the free grants. Furthermore, it wasn't really his department. "You are, of course, aware that it is neither desirable nor practicable that the Government should organize or attempt to control these societies or clubs; this must be done by Municipal or other local effort."[5] Carling suggested it was up to England to pay emigrants' expenses, as Canada had nothing to gain by doing so. Citing the fact that there were no guarantees that emigrants would stay in Canada once receiving financial aid, Carling reminded Herring that Canada's situation was quite different from that of Australia's and New Zealand's, as "Canada has a frontier bordering upon the United States for many hundreds of miles, which in many parts may be crossed in a few minutes...." Carling's slight indignation is a testament to the fact that the colonies never appreciated being told their business by representatives of the mother country. As affable as Herring seemed to be, he just may have overstepped diplomatic boundaries in lecturing a government minister.

Nevertheless, Herring was received with cheers from emigrants at the meetings he attended when he arrived back in Toronto from Muskoka. On October 17, he and Colonel Francis Cornwallis Maude attended a gathering at the Mechanics' Institute in the company of John Donaldson, the Toronto-based emigration agent. Of the many curious characters who appear in the free grant story, Colonel Maude, an English army officer who had been awarded the Victoria Cross for his actions in the Indian

Rebellion in 1857, was certainly one of the most eccentric. He must have cut a dashing figure in the backwoods. With his swirled waxed moustache, he looked every inch the English military man, perhaps somewhat out of place in the small rural community he chose as his home for two years. So taken was he with the free grant lands, he purchased several hundred acres in 1870 on Prospect Lake, just west of Gravenhurst. He was a major employer in the district, with a large staff for his country estate, and he had a propensity for leading hunting parties and entertaining lavishly. Thomas McMurray was a great admirer of Maude, and praised his emigration efforts, but Maude's time in Muskoka was short; in 1872 he returned to England, later becoming consul general in Warsaw.

At the Mechanics' Institute meeting, Herring talked generally about emigration and reported on his intention to visit Ottawa to try to solicit federal funds for emigration. Then Colonel Maude rose and corroborated Herring's comments, adding that emigrants would need at least £100 to settle successfully (which was at the high end of the range of the usual estimates), and that land settlement schemes were preferable to simply doling out money for would-be emigrants. He suggested that British emigrants preferred settling in Canada and other British colonies, rather than in the United States, although he warned that the States was actively recruiting emigrants in Britain. In conclusion, Maude predicted that Canada faced a "glorious future," and he was warmly applauded.

Herring returned to London with happy memories of Canada, but with the realization that not everyone was as enthusiastic about the free grants as he was. It was one thing to visit his old parishioners in settled areas of the province, where no doubt their lives had improved immeasurably. But there must have been doubts in his mind when he contemplated the lonely Muskoka wilderness. For the past few years, Herring had written letters to British newspapers, encouraging settlement in this country, but he was now expressing a measure of defensiveness. He sent one such letter to the *Belfast News-Letter* on November 9, 1870, written while he was in London, Ontario. "All at first experience troubles and difficulties, but after a short residence most are contented and happy. The number of those who disparage the good results of emigration are comparatively small and insignificant." He praised the free grant scheme, but complained, "The Government here [in Canada] is not quite alive to the great benefits of emigration, and they would do well to encourage it more liberally.... None need starve here. There are no workhouses or stone yards, and most of the inhabitants seem happy, contented, and prosperous." Perhaps Herring was still irritated by the missive of the previous March, in which the Reverend Thomas Hanson had had the audacity to attack the work of small emigration societies such as Herring's and to claim that emigrants were not doing well in Canada. Or maybe it still rankled when John Carling had gently admonished him for not understanding that municipal governments rather than provincial ones should be in charge of Canada-based emigration clubs. A week later, Herring wrote to the editor of the London *Times*, again extolling Canada as a destination for emigrants, and ensuring readers that 60 to 70 percent of the free grant land was fertile. Even Stephen Richards by this time had admitted that quite often up to half of a settler's free grant might not be arable, which was the reason he doubled the one hundred acres originally offered. Unfortunately, for the time being, Herring chose to ignore such admissions that Muskoka might not be ideal farming country.

On December 7, 1870, William Pearce Howland, Ontario's lieutenant governor, arrived at the Ontario Legislature escorted by Prime Minister John A. Macdonald and Lady Macdonald, as well as a troop of cavalry, to read the speech from the throne for the opening of the fourth session of the first Ontario Parliament. The speech was a self-congratulatory one, especially singling out the hard work of ministers in promoting emigration to the province. The *Globe's* December 8 editorial was critical of such claims. "We make bold to say that not five hundred immigrants have, during the past year, arrived in the Province through their influence. The distress in the East End of London and the persistent efforts of the benevolent in the old country are to be credited with the most of what has been accomplished." It's a safe bet that the *Globe* was referring to people such as Lady Hobart and Styleman Herring, but it could also be referring to another emigration philanthropist: around the same time, Maria Rye was "rescuing" poor children from the streets of East End London and bringing them to Canada. Although she was not directly involved in Muskoka settlement, undoubtedly some children ended up in the district.

Rye's methods were very different from Styleman Herring's, yet they were both active during the 1870s, with Rye carrying on until the end of the century. While Herring was insistent on state intervention in emigration both at home and in Canada, Rye openly scorned any such supervision. A short digression is in order here, as the work of Maria Rye reveals just how complicated the relationship was between emigration societies and the governments of the day.

Maria Rye was a notoriously difficult woman operating in what was then primarily a man's world. Her father, a solicitor, had a large family to support, so Rye, as an unmarried woman, was forced to make her own way in life. Her early career was as a journalist for Samuel Beeton's (husband and publisher of the popular Victorian cookbook writer, Mrs. Beeton) *Englishwoman's Domestic Magazine* and later for the *English Woman's Journal*. In 1862, she became a co-founder of the Female Middle Class Emigration Society, which sponsored the emigration of women to New Zealand. Rye's visit to that country with approximately one hundred emigrant women that same year was fraught with controversy: she was accused of running a sort of mail-order-bride business by bringing women who merely wished to find husbands rather than contribute to the country's economy through employment. In 1867, John Morrison, an emigration agent for Hawkes Bay, New Zealand, complained, "It is very difficult to deal with a Lady in business transactions. It is unwise of Miss Rye arguing that the rate of Passage money to New Zealand should not be more than to Australia."[6] Rye's reply was preciously coy: "I dont [*sic*] like Mr. Morrison ... he's a goose, — & what is worse he's a goose only to be managed by letting him have all his own way! wh. [which] I don't like at all!"[7] When she moved on to Australia in early 1863 to encourage Australian authorities to support female emigration, she again failed to make much impact other than to irritate the authorities.

Once back in England, Rye became an emigration agent in London and eventually turned her attention to Canada. In May 1868, she left Liverpool with a mix of single men and women, as well as families. But again she ran afoul of the authorities, especially William Dixon, the London-based agent-general for Canada, who accused Rye of taking to Canada women with "moral defects." And so, in 1869, Rye turned her attention solely to what she must have perceived as a more benign practice — child emigration. Unfortunately, Rye's "orphans" were often street children, many from London's East End, whom Rye was accused of scooping up at will, or the offspring of poorhouse dwellers, who were removed without their parents' permission. Rye set up Our Western Home, an orphanage in the Niagara region of Ontario, sending children out for adoption or fostering. However, unlike Herring, who seemed genuinely interested in the welfare of the emigrants he sent to Canada, Rye regarded the children she sent to Canada with a measure of disdain:

> Here is my "Black Book" — the Book of the replacement of my children, and the causes that have brought them back to the Home. You will see by this book that up to December, 1873, I have had 181 children returned to me, or have been removed by me for various causes, some for very trivial reasons, others for gross wickedness and immoralities. Many of the children, as you will see, have been placed by me 3, 4 and 5, and one 10 times over.[8]

Despite numerous accusations that she failed to keep proper records of the children in her care and often "misplaced" them, she ignored the authorities, insisting that she detested "red tape-ism," and was allowed to continue with her emigration scheme until 1896, when she retired and returned to England. Perhaps she anticipated the end when John Joseph Kelso, a prominent social reformer in Toronto, began to investigate child emigration schemes, an offshoot of his position as superintendent of neglected and dependent children in Ontario in the early 1890s. During the course of his investigations, he was critical of not only Rye's emigration methods, but of the woman herself. In his diary, a hand-written annotation reads, "Miss Rye did poor work — gave the girls to anyone, no subsequent supervision…. I had frequent clashes with her. Haughty lady — resented advice or criticism."[9] Although Rye rarely shrank from a good fight, it is more probable that her age was catching up with her: just seven years later, she died at the age of seventy-four. Despite her frequent run-ins with the authorities, she was encouraged for years by many who probably should have known better. Although she was supported by private citizens — specifically, Ontario farmers delighted to receive cheap, or free, domestic and agricultural labourers — Canadian authorities weren't too happy about being encumbered with Rye's pauper children. Perhaps Herring got on better with officials because he was always careful to send the "deserving poor" rather than paupers to Canada — and, of course, he didn't seem to have coerced his emigration club members to leave their homeland.

These two emigration schemes, Herring's and Rye's, are inextricably related, for they focused on people who in a large part lacked the power and the agency to determine the course of their own lives. They were at the mercy of government policies and benevolent philanthropists who took the liberty to shape their futures.

~

The year following Herring's visit to Canada, the free grant scheme was the source of a great deal of rancour, aimed in all directions. A *Globe* editorial on February 27, 1871, chastised Stephen Richards again for his stinginess with the free grant policy. "It was like breaking Stephen Richards on the wheel to secure any friendly concession for the good of the settlers, and had it not been for the outside pressure, the whole arrangements would have been very different from what they are to-day." To be sure that Richards got the message, the paper followed with a March 2 editorial that complained about his stinginess regarding timber rights for the free grant settlers. It concluded, "Mr. Richards is too old now to improve, and as an old fogy [*sic*] it is more than time he were laid on the shelf." Shaky grammar aside, the editorial implied that free grant settlers were hardly prospering; otherwise, why attack Richards so viciously? Incidentally, he was just around fifty years old at the time, maybe an old fogey by character, but not quite ready to be put out to pasture.

Richards wasn't the only one under attack that year. Thomas McMurray was singled out in a letter to the editor of the *Glasgow Herald* on June 29. The correspondent, "W.B.," quoted from a letter written to him by a fellow Scotsman — a surveyor and former farmer who had travelled to Canada with the idea of settling his family on a free grant of land. The friend was disappointed that the choicest lots were already taken, and as he was bent on a waterfront property, he had abandoned his plan for the time being. It could be that he had read glowing accounts of the land in McMurray's *Northern Advocate*, or even in McMurray's *Free Grant Lands of Canada*, which was published that year, for he wrote: "You have perhaps heard of Bracebridge and a Mr. McMurray — a pushing advocate of the free grants — himself a farmer, storekeeper, printer, and land agent. Now, as a practical Scotch farmer, I tell you plainly that there is no stretch of good soil in that neighbourhood. Spots there are of average quality, but if a particular survey does not show two-thirds of rock surface, then I claim no acquaintance with estimating areas and proportions. Bracebridge is McMurray, and McMurray is Bracebridge." The writer couldn't be faulted for his powers of observation, for indeed, McMurray did seem to have a finger in every pie.

Shortly after an annual federal government conference on emigration, the *Globe* grew increasingly cranky and mean-spirited. A September 28, 1871, editorial opined that Britain was far more active in publicizing emigration to Canada than were Canada's federal agents. In the mother country, emigration enthusiasts were forming emigration clubs and actively reporting on the subject in newspapers and journals. The *Globe* complained that James Moylan, an emigration agent stationed in Dublin in 1869, previous to Charles Foy, was "a broken-down political hack" but failed to mention what Moylan had done to deserve such condemnation. Another target was Christopher Dunkin, the head of the Bureau of Agriculture, Statistics, and Immigration, whose degrees from the universities of London, Glasgow, and Harvard failed to impress the editors of the paper. When Dunkin left his office that year to become a Quebec Supreme Court judge, the *Globe* deemed him "a total failure" in a scathing editorial on October 27. The author claimed that he had done nothing toward furthering immigration. Finally, he reminded readers that the census, which came under Dunkin's department, was still not completed, in contrast to Britain's and Australia's. Dunkin's replacement, John Henry Pope, a successful businessman, was described by the *Globe* as "a specimen of the most narrow-minded and contracted type of politician." Perhaps Pope was so described due to his cautionary approach to emigration — he felt Canada shouldn't overreach itself in attracting emigrants until the country had the necessary infrastructure. But more damning, perhaps, was the fact that among Pope's many business interests was the lumber trade, and the *Globe* spent much of the latter part of 1871 reporting on the conflicts between settlers and lumbermen on the free grant lands.

Perhaps the *Globe* was justified in criticizing these men, but one must remember that they faced a huge task: with limited funds they had to entice settlers to a young, largely undeveloped country, while competing with the much more sophisticated United States. And as the free grant lands were held as a major inducement to tempt British emigrants, it isn't surprising that government officials were slow to achieve optimum results, for during the next few years, they had to do battle with ever increasing attacks on the scheme.

～

On January 17, 1872, William Jeffrey Patterson, secretary of the Dominion Board of Trade in Ottawa, submitted to the board's annual general meeting a paper titled "Some Plain Statements About Immigration, and Its Results." Originally from Glasgow, Patterson had worked as a printer in the United States and later in Montreal, where he had been the secretary to the Montreal Board of Trade and the Montreal Corn Exchange Association before his appointment in 1870 to the Dominion board. The paper, published as a pamphlet soon after, wasn't good news for those singing the praises of backwoods life. "The experience of late years in the United States is, that new regions cannot be rapidly and efficiently settled, by individuals or single families plunging, so to speak, into the dense forest, and, axe in hand, hewing out their future destiny."[10] Not only was he against backwoods settlement, he was critical of societies that sent emigrants into the bush. "It must not be overlooked, however, that discretion on the part of the Emigration Agents in Europe is of incalculable importance. There must be discrimination exercised, — pauperised immigrants are not to be desired, — and perhaps much of the 'assisted' emigration should be discouraged. Every inducement should be given to those who have willing, hopeful hearts, strong arms, and good constitutions, to come hither and assist in laying, broad and deep, the foundations of civil and commercial prosperity."[11] Patterson believed that emigrants should come in organized parties, and that they should settle in centres with strong commercial and social infrastructures. He added that he could discuss particular schemes, presumably "assisted" ones, but was reluctant to do so. Whether or not Styleman Herring's would have been one of those singled out can only be conjectured.

~

In December 1871, John Sandfield Macdonald had been ailing and stepped down, with some nudging from Edward Blake, who replaced him. Blake, however, wasn't in power for long. In October 1872, it was decided that politicians could no longer serve as both federal and provincial representatives, and Blake chose federal politics. Oliver Mowat, Liberal member for Oxford North, stepped in as leader, and remained in office until 1896, thus being the longest-serving premier of the province to this day. Mowat was instrumental in devising further free grant schemes throughout his tenure, and by the end of his political career he had implemented the free land policy far into the province's northwest districts. Despite these changes of leadership in the early 1870s, encouraging emigration to Muskoka was still a top priority, and politicians strove to fine-tune the scheme in order to face down criticism.

In an effort to encourage further settlement, the Ontario government came up with the idea of offering a "refund bonus" of six dollars to unassisted emigrants — those who came to Canada on their own steam — and to those who sponsored new emigrants. There were two forms to be filled out before the bonus was awarded: the first to be completed by the person claiming the refund, and the second by a reliable sponsor, such as a mayor, reeve, emigration agent, clergyman, or employer. In a single-page handout compiled by David Spence, secretary for Ontario's Department of Immigration, it was advised: "Immigrants assisted out of this Province by any society or individual have no claim to the Refund; the same being payable only to the society or individual having so assisted them. No Refund is payable to any party who emigrated to Ontario previous to the year 1872." In other words, the assisted emigrant didn't receive the money, but his sponsor did. The Ontario Archives microfilm reels contain multiple requests to David Spence, some quite poignant, from settlers in the free grants who were desperately waiting for their refund, having encouraged a family member or friend to come to Canada. In fact, the whole idea may have been counterproductive as Spence had to weed through all the correspondence. Some letters were from obviously educated settlers and written in elegant copperplate. Others were untidy notes scribbled in barely decipherable English; their poignant requests for a mere six dollars were testaments to their desperate poverty.

There was confusion over the terms of the bonus as well. A letter appeared in the November 24, 1872, edition of *Lloyd's Weekly Newspaper* appealing to the editor as "a friend of the emigrant." "A Clerk," as the correspondent identified himself, complained that his son had canvassed Styleman Herring's Clerkenwell society for help to emigrate. Herring requested £6 5s. for costs and the son paid up immediately. Of course, even assisted emigrants were asked to pay a little way toward their passage, although "A Clerk" didn't seem to realize this. The son claimed to have been told, having arrived in Canada, that the government would pay six dollars to unassisted emigrants, and of course he considered himself to be one of them. However, when he applied for the bonus he was told that the money had been remitted to Herring. The correspondent claimed to have consulted Herring, who suggested that the bonus would be paid out by the Canadian government. Herring may have been misinformed, too, but it is more likely the correspondent's son was either ignorant of the rules, or attempting to play fast and loose with the authorities. Either way, the bonus was an obvious headache and may have done little to encourage emigration.

~

In the autumn of 1873, two Englishmen arrived in Canada in order to assess the country as a destination for emigrating farmworkers in Britain. Joseph Arch was the founder and president of Britain's National Agricultural Labourers' Union, and had been a farmer and later a lay preacher before he became involved in promoting the welfare of low-paid farmers in Britain. Arthur Clayden was a journalist who served on the union's advisory consulting committee, and had been an emigration agent in New Zealand before he joined Arch's NALU. In Britain, most agricultural land was traditionally owned by the wealthy, and farmers generally were hired at low wages or they rented small plots with little yield. Although the union members believed that the farmers' working conditions should be improved in England, which would prevent them from having to emigrate, they conceded that landowners were reluctant to raise wages or improve conditions. Therefore, Arch and Clayden were delegated to journey to Canada to seek out agricultural opportunities for emigrants. Clayden sent regular reports of his journey to London's

Daily News, and a compilation of these articles appeared in a chapter of his book *Revolt of the Field*, which was published the following year.

Clayden claimed that he was not altogether comfortable endorsing emigration for Britain's farmworkers — he believed that those individuals willing to farm, for higher wages, the vast empty spaces in northern regions of the country should be able to make a decent living in the familiar surroundings of home. However, he was willing to assess the possibility of emigration to the colony that so many Britons now called home. Clayden and Arch received quite the welcome in Canada: they were invited by Lord Dufferin, the governor general, to the Citadel in Quebec City, where he was staying temporarily. In Ottawa, they met representatives of the agricultural department. Clayden's assessment of John Henry Pope, the new head of the Bureau of Agriculture, Immigration, and Statistics, was more complimentary than that of the *Globe*'s: he described Pope as "a shrewd, practical, and exceedingly intelligent public officer."[12] Upon meeting Prime Minister John A. Macdonald, Clayden confided that the leader looked remarkably like Benjamin Disraeli, at that time the rather flamboyant Conservative leader of the Opposition in Britain's House of Commons.[13] They joined Oliver Mowat and "various other Canadian celebrities" in Toronto, and then took a little time out for a sightseeing visit to Niagara Falls. Their itinerary is familiar even today for anyone who has visited Ontario's star attraction: Clayden admired Brock's Monument at Queenston Heights, rhapsodized over the churning Niagara River and the mists arising from the falls, and confided that Canada's Horseshoe Falls were vastly superior to those on the American side. With much trepidation, he descended the precarious steps that led to the Cave of the Winds, from which he viewed the cascading water overhead.

After travelling throughout the Niagara region, stopping at St. Catharines and Hamilton, they reached Gravenhurst on October 3. Clayden described the town as a "straggling sort of village — I beg the Canadians' pardon, I should have said town — on the side of the beautiful bay of Muskoka. Here a steamer took us across the bay and up the picturesque river Muskoka some twelve miles to Bracebridge, another Canadian 'town.' Nothing could exceed the exquisite beauty of the river, which winds like a serpent, and of the autumnal tints of its thickly-wooded [*sic*] sides. The town was disappointing. It consisted of a few straggling wooden buildings, and streets which were mud tracks. The people were ragged and haggard-looking."[14] Clayden, who hearkened from a land of quaint little villages, was appalled by the reality of the free grant frontier. As if to stress the wild nature of the free grant district, he added a little drama to his story by relating his conversation with a farmer who, nine years previously, had had to fight off a violent attack by an "Indian" who had challenged his right to settle in Native territory. According to many settlers' accounts, Aboriginal-settler encounters were largely peaceful, even friendly: Clayden would later be chastised for suggesting otherwise.

Upon reaching Huntsville, he was brutally honest. "Anything more desolate than that wild track through the forest I cannot conceive. The hundred acres of land given to settlers are a sort of white elephant to the unfortunate recipients. The donation drags them down to the very verge of barbarism.... The truth is, none but the hardiest and most persevering men can do any good in these wild regions, and they must lay their account for years of 'roughing it.'"[15] He simply couldn't fathom a British farmer settling there, for at home they had "social comforts and advantages which I look in vain for among the scattered shanties of these Canadian forests."[16]

And then, a few paragraphs later, Clayden did a slight turnabout: perhaps uncomfortable with his findings, he scrambled to soften his negative report, no doubt mindful that the government representatives he had met might not be too happy with his assessment of the free grant lands. Throughout his journey, he had remarked on the beauty of the Muskoka landscape, something he could turn to advantage. "I scarcely wonder that amid all their hardships the settlers shrink from the thought of leaving their forest home. After all, it is their own, and they are wholly unfettered by the conventionalisms of society."[17] Confident that he had finished on a positive note, and despite the poverty, barbarism, and desolation that he had just described, he helpfully suggested that Mr. Arch would probably bring one hundred men out to the free grant lands the following year, if the government helped with building homes, clearing land, and finding employment for settlers who were short of funds.

On October 25, the *Liverpool Mercury* published an article Clayden had written for the *Labourers' Union Chronicle*. He admitted that "[f]ew things have given Mr. Arch more trouble than his investigation of these said free grant lands, and their eligibility for his fellow labourers." And yet he then went on with the usual sentiment that *hardworking* settlers in Muskoka had a chance at success. However, readers of his reports were already taking issue with his findings. On October 28, in a letter to the *Daily Mail*, Sydney Robjohns, an Ontario emigration officer based in London, England, ridiculed Clayden's report, especially his description of war-like Indians. "A man going over Hampstead-heath might as reasonably be apprehensive of molestation from Greek banditti, as a settler at Bracebridge of an attack of Red men." Robjohns admitted he had witnessed a ceremonial Indian "war dance," but he felt it must have seemed as incongruous to the Natives as it would have to the settlers.

Arch and Clayden returned from Canada on November 18, and on November 21, a reporter from the *Birmingham Daily Post* visited Arch at his home in the picturesque village of Barford, on the road between Warwick and Stratford-Upon-Avon. Although weary from his ocean journey, Arch graciously sat down for an interview, and was open about his criticism of Muskoka's free grant lands. He claimed that the land was "laid out very injudiciously," and that the provincial government was totally unsympathetic when Arch suggested settlers should have rights to timber on their land. The government had told him that for the past fifty years settlers had "made their own way." But civilization had advanced since then, Arch argued, and it was ridiculous to stick to a policy that hurt the settlers. He thought of Canada as an ideal destination for the members of his farmworkers' union, but favoured the fertile land around London, Ontario. Following the interview with Arch, the paper published a letter by Clayden, who denied accusations that the Canadian government had tried to "hoodwink and bamboozle" them. Apart from the free grants, he also expressed confidence in the new country of Canada.

By this time, Arch and Clayden must have begun to regret their visit, as the controversy continued to dog them. The December 16, 1873, issue of London's *Daily Mail* featured a letter from Clayden, who was probably fed up with defending himself. He included some correspondence sent to him from a free grant settler of three years' standing, who was also the author of the quote that began this chapter. Obviously written by an educated person, the letter pulled no punches. The anonymous (or Clayden chose not to publish his name) correspondent wrote: "I have lived three years in the Free Grants — have chopped, cleared, split rails, sowed and reaped, and gone through all the heat and burden of the day.... The *Globe* ... pretends that in those barren wastes the labours and privations of the settlers are only what all Ontario pioneers have gone through. Bosh! ... The soil of this vast area is nearly all sand and rocks, with occasional spots of clay and limestone." Pointing out that "nothing worth anything is ever given away," he went on to note that "it would need the pen of a Fielding or Dickens adequately to set forth the life of the unhappy Englishman entrapped into these rocky and sandy wastes." In Muskoka, he reminded Clayden, settlers met a number of hardships, including the harsh climate, grasshoppers, mosquitoes, black flies, droughts, and bad roads. Clayden may have felt uncomfortable revealing the letter's next words, for the settler then went on to call into question the integrity of not only the well-regarded Styleman Herring, but also a Congregationalist minister, the splendidly named Horrocks Cocks. "Men like Mr. Cocks or Mr. Herring take a brief pleasure jaunt in company with a Cabinet Minister or land speculator, whose whole object is to get the country settled, and return 'delighted with all they have seen and heard,' having heard and seen in reality only what some smart person intended they should hear and see."

We are well acquainted with Styleman Herring, but what of this new character in our free grant story? In 1871, Horrocks Cocks had made an informal deal with John Carling that he would lecture in England on the benefits of emigration to Canada and would be reimbursed for his expenses. After Carling resigned as commissioner of agriculture and public works later that year, Archibald McKellar succeeded him. To Cocks's dismay, McKellar neglected to respond to his letters requesting that he make good on Carling's deal. On January 11, 1872, Cocks pointed out to McKellar that "The States are moving heaven and earth *here*, and Canada is doing *next to nothing.*"[18] He reminded McKellar that his time was valuable and in a postscript wrote: "My proposition was not an extravagant one. The very opposite." Eventually, McKellar hired him in November 1872, as the chief commissioner of emigration for Ontario in England and Wales at a salary of $150 per year plus travelling expenses, but he was abruptly dismissed shortly after. Cocks seemed to have been a constant irritant to the authorities, although he did find a champion in the Toronto *Globe*, which, in a lengthy editorial on April 11, 1873, expressed grave doubts that Cocks had been dismissed from the Russell House in Ottawa due to intoxication!

And so we return to the final words of the anonymous settler's letter to Arthur Clayden on December 16, in which he concluded with excerpts from the *St. Mary's Vidette* editorial that Thomas McMurray had printed in his *Free Grant Lands* guide. He then tacked on an excerpt from the *Seaforth Expositor*, which read: "Those who have settled in Muskoka are dragging out a miserable existence, and only remain because they have not the means to leave." Clayden may have been reluctant to besmirch the names of Herring and Cocks, but he obviously did not want to be tarred by the same brush. He assured readers once again that he had no reservations about emigration to Canada in general, just not to the free grant lands. Horrocks Cocks wasn't about to be insulted, however. He dashed off a reply to the *Birmingham Daily Post*, which was published December 20. Cocks accused the settler Clayden had quoted as being a disappointed one who had lacked foresight in settling the free grants. And yet, Cocks admitted that he did agree with the settler partly. "The idea of sending 10,000 families, or even 1,000, in any one year, to settle in Muskoka as farmers, is not only preposterous, but monstrous, unless, indeed, they be the hardy race I have mentioned."

Finally, by the close of 1873, in a missive to the London *Times*, Clayden responded to a letter that had appeared a few days before from a Mr. W. Brown, a land surveyor based in Orillia, who chastised him for exaggerating problems in Muskoka. In a reply dated December 27, Clayden patiently set out his arguments, assuring Brown that there were some good farming areas in Muskoka, but, in the spirit of Oliver Cromwell's instructions to his portraitist, he had intended to "paint warts and all." He then added a letter written to him by a clergyman acting as a missionary in Muskoka, who claimed that strong endorsements of Muskoka were emanating from the more well-to-do settlers, and told only half the story. "The half has not been told — the half of hardship, privation, and wretchedness; but the poorest labourer in England is far better off, far more comfortable, and ... might be far more happy.... Many of these settlers have told me that such a life is not life, but only a mere existence."

Chapter Six

Styleman Herring's Defection

It is certain, too, that the endeavours which are often made to pack off shiploads of Emigrants from England are not made in the interest of those who are sent out, and that they lead continually to great sufferings and disappointments.[1]
— London *Times* editorial, 1874

The controversy over Arch and Clayden's findings continued into 1874 in both the British and Canadian press. Just after the New Year, the *Globe* didn't hesitate to discredit Arch and Clayden's report, which had immediately made headlines both at home and abroad. On January 7, 1874, the paper ran an editorial concerning the settler whose correspondence with Arthur Clayden had been published in the *Daily Mail*. That settler had been highly critical not just of the free grant district, but of Styleman Herring, Horrocks Cocks, John Edward Jennings, and the Duke of Manchester, all of whom he accused of having been tricked by their government hosts into supporting the free grants. The *Globe* identified, but didn't name, the settler as a well-known figure in Muskoka, a man who was a "chronic grumbler." According to the editorial, this settler had taken up a free grant lot that had been abandoned by others due to its poor fertility and had had the arrogance to believe he would be much more successful than they had been. The *Globe* defended its position: "We have no wish to represent any part of our country as better than it is. Such a proceeding would be foolish and short-sighted in the extreme, for it would injure the cause we seek to promote, and the country in whose welfare we take the deepest interest." The *Globe*'s concern for the country's future may have been admirable, but its lack of sympathy for the welfare of Muskoka's struggling settlers reflected the attitude of most free grant supporters.

That same day, January 7, Arthur Clayden was embroiled in his own battle. A few days before, he had been rebuked by William Drogo Montagu, the seventh Duke of Manchester,[2] who had recently visited Muskoka. With the exception of one couple whom he regarded as unsuited for the rigours of farming the free grants, he found the landscape to be beautiful and the settlers content. Clayden patiently explained in a letter to the editor of the *Times* that his goal in travelling to Muskoka had not been to take in the scenery, and pointed out that Richard William Scott, the commissioner of Crown lands in Ontario, had recently informed the Legislature that "Some years ago I made a calculation and found there were 2,000 settlers on those [free grant colonization] roads. Five years afterwards 1,600 of these families, placed there at considerable expense, had abandoned the country." Although Scott rather confusingly compared numbers of individual settlers with numbers of families, his observation suited Clayden's intention to defend himself against the duke's rebuke. The following day, a correspondent named James Wilson took issue with Clayden, pointing out that although he "had no personal knowledge of Muskoka," he observed that Clayden had mentioned "the autumnal tints of maple, ash, and basswood.... Now, everybody in Canada knows that maple only grows on the richest soil." Clayden responded on January 12 with some sarcasm: "I regret that one so evidently fitted to instruct us on a subject is thus of little use in the discussion which is really occupying our attention." Then he amended his initial comment, explaining that maples were actually scarce in Muskoka, and there was more pine and scrubby oak.

R.J. Oliver, the Crown land agent based in Orillia who had been handing out location tickets for colonization of the Muskoka Road even before the free grant scheme had been initiated, entered the fray. He blasted Clayden in a letter published on March 21, 1874, in the *Royal Cornwall Gazette* (and other British papers as well). "It was unfortunate, nay, foolish, in [*sic*] Mr. Clayden to launch upon a subject on which he was so lamentably ignorant.

His flying visit to Muskoka gave him no information as to the condition of the settlers, the quality of the land, or the nature of bush farming." Oliver was disgusted that Clayden had made these observations having been in Muskoka only "for one day." Actually, Clayden had arrived in Muskoka on October 3, and wrote from Huntsville on October 5, so to give him credit, he was there for at least a few days. After all the work he had done to promote Muskoka for settlement, Oliver obviously wasn't about to have some upstart from Britain undo all that he had accomplished.

~

In Bracebridge, Thomas McMurray was having his own problems. The depression that had begun in the United States in 1873 was being felt even in the Canadian backwoods, and as his businesses failed, he was forced to declare bankruptcy in July 1874. At least he had been able to keep busy despite his money troubles — he had published *Temperance Lectures* in 1873 in Toronto, reflecting his boyhood passion. But McMurray wasn't about to be defeated: he sold his *Northern Advocate* and moved back to Parry Sound after his businesses collapsed and started up another newspaper, the *North Star*, which presumably gave him a continued platform for his advocacy of the free grants. This must have been a difficult time for him. He had invested so much effort into building up Bracebridge, as well as the free grant scheme. He also faced competition from the *Free Grant Gazette*, a Liberal paper published out of Bracebridge. In his heyday, McMurray had built an impressive downtown three-storey office building in Bracebridge, which seemed to have exemplified his success. But when W.E. Hamilton arrived in the town in the spring of 1875, the "fine brick block" was boarded up. He consulted his landlord at the North American Hotel to find out what had happened to McMurray's business. Hamilton learned that McMurray's "downfall knocked the bottom out of the institution of Bracebridge."[3] McMurray, he noted, had possessed "a great deal of the live go-ahead yankee [sic] dealing about him."[4] The shop, which had formerly been successful enough to require five clerks, left a void in the Bracebridge business community. Like many other buildings hastily erected in the frontier town, McMurray's was constructed poorly, and it was razed shortly after he left for Parry Sound. According to Geraldine Coombe, author of *Muskoka Past and Present*, there were some in town who felt McMurray had rather overreached himself in building such a showy building.⁵ Nevertheless, McMurray probably didn't let any lingering resentments bother him. He was an old hand at reinventing himself, and probably enjoyed making a fresh start in Parry Sound

Muskoka settlers had some relief from their troubles when Lord and Lady Dufferin, the governor general and his wife, visited the district during the summer of 1874. Dufferin was committed to being a hands-on governor general, and strove to meet Canadians on their home ground by travelling extensively throughout the country. Whether celebrating the coming of the railway or welcoming a passel of dignitaries, Muskoka's residents certainly knew how to put on a good show. When the governor general reached Gravenhurst on July 27, it seems the whole town turned out to take part in the festivities. The following report from the Orillia *Times* on August 6 gives us a wonderful opportunity to witness life in a small Victorian Ontario town:

The true and loyal subjects of Her Majesty Queen Victoria, living in and near this place, were to-day cheered by a sight of the representative of that Sovereign and great was the enthusiasm in consequence. Too much cannot be said in praise of the taste and energy with which the arrangements for the reception were carried out. The principal object of attraction was a large archway flanked by two smaller ones, and composed of pine boughs — fitting emblems of Muskoka. The principal arch was surmounted by a crown, below which on the south side were the words "Welcome to Muskoka," and on the north side "God save the Queen...." A little further on a splendid banner stretched completely across the street leading toward the wharf, with "Welcome Lord and Lady Dufferin."⁶

Lady Dufferin described her trip to Muskoka in her diary, *My Canadian Journal*, and her observations can lead us to believe that the visit, like Styleman Herring's and Charles Marshall's, had been carefully orchestrated. She was able to interview a "very charming emigrant," a woman who had been a lady's maid on the estate of Sir William and Lady

Anna Stirling-Maxwell, where her husband had been the valet. Although they had known nothing about farming, the family was prospering, thanks to the fertility of their free grant land. The emigrant was "so merry, and so happy and courageous,"[7] Lady Dufferin reported. As she travelled on to Rosseau, Lady Dufferin encountered some very poor Icelanders, but later, on her way to Parry Sound, she ran into a farming family whose nine children were decked out in white frocks and sashes. This seems odd attire for the backwoods, which suggests that the visit was planned beforehand by authorities who were anxious for her to see only the positive side of free grant settlement. She made no mention of any difficulties that free grant land settlers might be having, although she did note that many lots were quite rocky.

~

During the summer of 1874, the free grant scheme was a prominent subject in the British press. On June 23, a correspondent who identified himself as "Irish-American" wrote to the *Belfast News-Letter*, sparking a prolonged debate. The writer had travelled to Canada two years before to take up a free grant of land, but he was not impressed with what he saw. "The free grant land district of Muskoka was said to resemble the Garden of Eden in fertility. I will only say that if the 'holding' of our first parents bore any resemblance to Muskoka we can forgive them for eating the forbidden fruit. The place is appropriately called the 'Wilderness,' and such a wild, barren, uninhabited, uncultivated tract of country one could hardly imagine." "Irish-American" had relocated to Pittsburgh and was gainfully employed, grateful to escape the free grant lands.

Charles Foy, Canada's emigration agent based in Belfast, was outraged at the comments made by "Irish-American" and addressed them in a correspondence to the editor of the *Belfast News-Letter* on June 24, 1874. "In the *News-Letter* of this day I read the letter of an 'Irish-American,' and his amusing — no doubt he thought it amusing — account of the free grant district of Muskoka. In fair play, I ask insertion of the opinions of Marshall, a writer whose independence cannot be questioned." Foy then quoted from Charles Marshall's *The Canadian Dominion*, specifically the encounter in Muskoka in 1870 between Styleman Herring and his former parishioners, who were thrilled at meeting their old friend.

Surely, Foy suggested, this was proof that "Irish-American" was wrong in his assessment of the free grants. "Irish-American" was simply "a fool." As Canada's representative, Foy would naturally feel he had to defend the free grant district, but Marshall's account, describing a journey taken in 1870, was hardly an up-to-date description of the free grant lands.

In July 24, 1874, a letter to the London *Times* sparked further debate over the desirability of emigration to Canada and, later, to the free grant lands specifically. The correspondent, "A Bohemian," was an Englishman who had arrived in Canada in the spring of 1870, having tried and failed to settle in New Zealand. He reported that the British emigrants he encountered were dissatisfied with Canada, and that they laboured for low wages on farms in a country with a short growing season. He claimed that "the vast majority of Canadian immigrants are merely hewers of wood and drawers of water." In another letter on August 11, he continued to describe his Canadian experience. Initially he had worked as a reporter for a daily newspaper, but the wages were as poor as his shorthand, and he eventually found employment as a police officer in Toronto. Describing meetings with emigrants who were leading a miserable existence, he maintained that when winter arrived there was "no work, no comfort, no home; only wretched shanties to live in, and no hope of obtaining anything like an independence."

On the following day, Styleman Herring responded to the comments made by "A Bohemian" in a letter to the *Times*, but suddenly, it seemed, Herring had reversed his earlier advocacy of the free grant scheme. He pointed out that he had visited Canada at the same time as "A Bohemian" and had found, for the most part, his emigrants were doing well. Since returning to Britain, he had received "joyful and grateful letters" from many of them. But then he casually announced: "I freely confess [that] since last Fall matters have been gloomy in the Dominion, and, consequently, our society has of late aided most to New Zealand." *New Zealand?* Had he been wooed by emigration authorities there? He doesn't seem to have visited the country. His reasons for deserting Canada were not really clear, although certainly the depression of the mid-1870s was a reality. But wasn't he taking an even greater risk to turn suddenly to faraway New Zealand as a home for emigrants? The reasons for Herring's decision remain largely a mystery. Had he left behind diaries or personal correspondence, we might have learned why he had such a turn of heart.[8] He did rather cryptically explain his decision in January 1875, in an article in the *Victoria Magazine*: "Years ago my attention was turned to Canada as a field for emigration; but there are many hindrances to it.... With regards to New Zealand, I prefer to send emigrants there; it offers greater advantages, and I have not lately sent many to Canada."[9]

Canadian emigration authorities would have ascertained by then that all was not well: in 1873, Herring sent about twenty parties over to Canada; in 1874, the passenger ship lists indicated that he sent a total of *eleven people*. These emigrants sailed between April and August, on six different ships. His sponsorship of eleven people hardly qualified as an emigration "scheme." Presumably he simply aided the odd parishioner who wished to join family or friends in Canada. By the spring of 1874, the time of year emigrants usually began to arrive, emigration authorities must have realized that Herring's interest in Canada had waned. Herring softened his announcement by ensuring readers in the *Times* that his emigrants enjoyed Canada's healthy weather, school system, open employment opportunities, and high wages, but then finished with what was the death knell of his Muskoka advocacy. Emigrants still wishing to go to Canada should try Manitoba, which, he claimed, was the best place for people with a little capital. Muskoka's free grant scheme no longer figured in on Herring's agenda.

Reaction to Herring's letter was swift. John Edward Jenkins, who had replaced William Dixon as the agent-general for Canada in London, was not amused. The day following Herring's letter, he wrote to the *Times*, dismissing the observations of "A Bohemian" and then attacking Herring's take on the gloomy matters in the Dominion. "I cannot understand to what he refers. The gloom is in his spectacles." Jenkins claimed that Americans were currently flooding into Canada, and he added that "the Press has recently teemed with a series of active, angry, and apparently concerted attacks on Canada." On a trip back to England on the *Polynesian*, he recalled meeting on board "a weak, lymphatic creature, with a dried-up wife and six children, whose faces had broken out in scrofulous sores." This family was from London's East End, the main source of Herring's emigrant pool. The connection becomes clear in Jenkins's conclusion that, "[In] spite of our efforts, numbers of such people will go out, helped out often by good souls, whose charity, unfortunately, not only begins at home, but goes abroad with the object of it." In other words, if philanthropists such as Herring send out emigrants who were in need of charity at home, chances were that they would continue to require charity in their adopted country.

On August 13, James Crabtree, a stonecutter from Muskoka, weighed in to the debate in the *Times*. Attempting to dissuade his fellow countrymen — Crabtree hailed from Birmingham — from coming to Canada to "better their condition," he warned specifically against the free grant district. "The books and papers circulated in England about this country are a pack of lies.... The land is barely covered with a few inches of light soil; in fact, it should not be called land, for it is all rock (granite) for many hundred miles, with pine trees growing wherever there is a chance. I wish to Heaven some of those agents in England were sent out here just for one twelvemonth to chop wood and live in the bush; they would not be so anxious to get poor men and their families to leave dear old England."

On August 15, "B" from Berkshire, who had visited Canada in 1873 with the intent of investing his capital in a farming enterprise, gave a corroborating account of settlement on the free grants, complaining about the black flies and mosquitoes and the general unsuitability of the land. He also questioned the basic premise of the Free Grants Act, by which emigrants could become owners of their land. "Why is it that all labouring men who emigrate indulge in the visionary fancy of becoming what is called in England 'landed proprietors'? It is very difficult to connect the phrase in one's mind with the ague-stricken and fly-bitten inhabitants of the distant and dismal tracts of rock and lake known and posted at the English railway stations as the 'free grant settlements.'" It would be far better, he asserted, to work for an established farmer and receive £40 including board and lodging. In fact, if emigrants were determined to go to Canada, they should look for land in Manitoba, he concluded, echoing Herring's suggestion. "B" scoffed at those who wished to ape the landowning gentry of Britain: there was nothing wrong in working for a good wage for others.

Four days later, on August 19, J.S. Lawrie, who gave the Whitehall Club as his address, wrote of his experience in Canada:

We shortly found that the idea of accepting, even as a gift, the land commonly offered on the most alluring terms to the enterprising emigrant was illusory in the extreme. Not only were such grants of land too far distant from an accessible market, but the labour of clearing the surface from "soft lumber" (a sure index of unproductive soil) would have consumed at least two years, or nearly all the capital which an average emigrant farmer has at his disposal, even supposing his spirits and strength survived so severe a test of industry, accompanied by the natural drawbacks of unusually protracted winters.

With such dismal reports of the free grant district landing on the editor's desk, the *Times* printed its own point of view on August 21:

What is most needed is strength of limb and willingness both to work and to put up with hardships, and the man who is thus qualified for success may take his passage to Canada without much fear that he will be left long unemployed.... If he is determined to be his own master and not to work for hire, he had better pay for good land in an available situation than accept as a free gift the kind of allotment which would be assigned to him.... It is certain, too, that the endeavours which are often made to pack off shiploads of Emigrants from England are not made in the interest of those who are sent out, and that they lead continually to terrible sufferings and disappointments.

Undoubtedly, Styleman Herring, who had devoted so much energy to "packing off shiploads" of emigrants to the colonies, would have been furious reading the editorial, for it virtually discredited his work of the past six years. It was one thing to criticize Muskoka as an unsuitable destination for agricultural emigration, but it was quite another to attack those benevolent philanthropists who had only the emigrants' best interests in mind. Herring probably even harboured some un-Christian-like feelings toward his Canadian hosts of 1870 who had encouraged him to send his parishioners and others to a district that was evidently not suited for farming. Visions of Muskoka rock must have haunted him; he had been simply lied to by his hosts and was now put into a humiliating position. It would have been embarrassing to admit that he had been duped by the premier of Ontario and his fellow hosts. Herring could hardly have been a happy man reading the *Times* that August.

A few days after the editorial appeared, "A Bohemian," maybe sensing he had initiated the controversy over emigration to Canada, wished to balance his views on emigration with "the bright side of the picture." He now addressed the sunnier side of emigration to Canada, but warned, "I have much more to say concerning agricultural life in Canada, which to the wealthy is one of the most delightful pictures that can be imagined, but the poor, the maimed, the halt, and the blind are in a far more pitiable state than is ever experienced in this country." He followed this rather backhanded compliment three days later, on August 24, with a warning: "As to 'free grants of land to poor emigrants,' it is all moonshine." He included a condensed version of the Free Grants Act, then followed up with:

> I have no desire to comment upon these terms [of the Free Grants Act], except to tell you that the lands offered free are all far away in the back woods, through which there are no roads and no neighbours, and that should a man accept a hermit's life such as this he must take with him provisions, tools, &c., to last him a considerable time before he gets any return for his labour, and the only visitor who comes near him will be the tax-gatherer; for do not let it be supposed that the "free land" is untaxed; no! [H]e has to pay $10 a year toward the Local Government expenses for every 100 acres allotted to him, and if he has not means to do this the allotment is taken from him.

He concluded by answering Jenkins's complaint that "A Bohemian" was hiding under a nom du plume. He preferred not to reveal his identity but included his address at the end of the letter, ensuring readers that he was pleased to provide evidence on his findings in Canada. Herring fought back, but rather than defending his own involvement in the free grant scheme, he wisely pointed the finger at the state. On August 26, he wrote:

> "A Bohemian's" letter of yesterday gives a much more cheering and, in my experience, accurate view of emigration generally.... I would, Sir, to-day ask, is emigration profitable to the nation at large? Is our present system the best that can be adopted? And is our Government Emigration Office quite up to the present requirements? ... Thanks to the goodness and care of the mothers in England we increase at the rate of 1,000 each day, and I contend that colonization is an essential offshoot for our ever-increasing population, and to desert our Colonies would be a suicidal policy.... And, finally, the Government Emigration Office requires more life-vigour and to have means granted to it to carry out emigration to our Colonies, for at present it emigrates nobody.

After all the energy Herring had spent leading delegations to the Poor Law Board, speaking at colonization committees, and crossing the ocean to view Canada, specifically the remote free grant district, he knew who the laggards were. If anyone had shown "life-vigour," it was he. His frustration was evident, and he was courageous enough to speak publicly. Luckily, the debate rather fizzled out after August, so at least Herring could get on with his life without the constant reminder that the free grant scheme hadn't quite panned out as he had hoped.

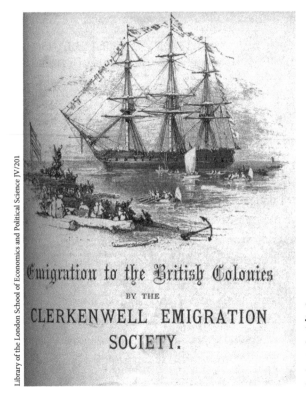

Styleman Herring's 1870 emigration pamphlet, Emigration to the British Colonies by the Clerkenwell Emigration Society, *with the evocative image of an emigration ship as it sets sail to cross the Atlantic.*

Styleman Herring's home and the office for the Clerkenwell Emigration Society in the borough of Islington, London, at 45 Colebrooke Row. The house is a short stroll from the Regent's Canal, and several blocks north of the poorer parish of St. Paul's, Clerkenwell.

THE

FREE GRANT LANDS

OF

CANADA,

FROM PRACTICAL EXPERIENCE OF BUSH FARMING IN THE
FREE GRANT DISTRICTS OF

MUSKOKA AND PARRY SOUND

BY

THOS. McMURRAY, J. P.,

ONE OF THE FIRST SETTLERS IN DRAPER, AND EX-REEVE OF THE UNITED
TOWNSHIPS OF DRAPER, MACAULAY STEPHENSON, ETC., ETC.

BRACEBRIDGE, ONT., CANADA :

PRINTED AND PUBLISHED AT THE OFFICE OF THE "NORTHERN ADVOCATE."
1871.

The title page of Thomas McMurray's Free Grant Lands of Canada, *the most
comprehensive book on the free grant scheme of Muskoka and Parry Sound.*

THE RESIDENCE OF   "THE GROVE,"
BRACEBRIDGE.   THOS. MCMURRAY. ESQ.

Thomas McMurray's grand mansion, which stood near the current high school in Bracebridge. The Grove epitomized the lofty heights that successful settlers could aspire to.

The idyllic log cabin featured in the April 1869 issue of the Ontario Farmer, and reproduced in the 1871 edition of the Ontario government's Emigration to Canada: the Province of Ontario *guide for new settlers.*

45 Colebrooke Row N
March 30

My Lord

The distress which prevails in agricultural & other places has brought forth a large number of poor but suitable persons most anxious for Emigration, wh the late Archbishop of Canterbury said was "The embodiment of practical Xtianity." The success — during the past 14 years in aiding 4500 people to the Colonies — and the prosperity of the majority — has proved that it is the most permanent way of helping the poor. We now stand greatly in need of funds and hoping you will generously assist these poor people

I remain Y. Obd.
A. Styleman Herring
Vicar and Chairman

St. Pauls
Clerkenwell.

From the author's collection

Styleman Herring's request for emigration funds from Lord Doneraile of County Cork, Ireland. The note is simply dated "March 30," but as Herring writes that he has been aiding emigrants for the past fourteen years, it was likely written around 1882, the year of his second visit to Canada. The text reads:

My Lord, The distress which prevails in agricultural & other places has brought forth a large number of poor but suitable persons most anxious for Emigration, wh [sic] the late Archbishop of Canterbury said was "The embodiment of practical Xtianity." The success — during the past 14 years in aiding 4500 people to the Colonies — and the prosperity of the majority — has proved that it is the most permanent way of helping the poor. We now stand greatly in need of funds and hoping you will generously assist these poor people.

A page of W. E. Hamilton's 1879 Guide Book & Atlas of Muskoka and Parry Sound, showing Stephenson Township. Amid the sea of settlers' names is Harriet Barbara King's and her family.

Chapter Seven

Winners and Losers

It is a wild country hereabouts, and utterly valueless for agricultural purposes, although here and there a clearing has been made, evidently to little purpose, as many of the places seem deserted.[1]
— John Clay, *New World Notes*

Despite the dire reports on emigration that flooded the British press in 1874, by 1875 Muskoka's towns and villages were thriving, with small industries and businesses providing a degree of prosperity. On January 1, Bracebridge became an incorporated village, enabling the burgeoning community to manage its own affairs. Although certainly affected by the economic depression in the United States, the town became the nucleus of business activity in the district. As well, smaller towns and villages such as Gravenhurst, Huntsville, Rosseau, Port Carling, and Uffington were more than holding their own. Even Lancelot, the tiny hamlet where Harriet Barbara King settled, was described by Enid Brown in her history of Stephenson Township as quite "lively" in the 1870s, although today *lively* would hardly describe the remote and almost deserted community. Another sign of the district's growing maturity was the abolition in Bracebridge of statute labour; now the municipal government became responsible for road building, thus freeing the settlers from this onerous obligation. The institution of local agricultural societies and fall fairs was another indication that some of the district's farmers were meeting with success. In other words, all was not gloom and doom in Muskoka. As these towns kept the district's economic engines running, another source of income was becoming entrenched in Muskoka: a burgeoning tourist industry. Long before the Free Grants Act was passed, sportsmen and tourists had discovered the region as a recreational destination, but as transportation networks improved by the 1870s, Muskoka's tourist industry grew rapidly.

For decades, Ontario's landscapes had drawn visitors who were looking for a wilderness experience. In her book *Wild Things: Nature, Culture, and Tourism in Ontario, 1790–1914*, Patricia Jasen traced the peregrinations of early tourists throughout the province as they marvelled at its romantic features. As early as the 1790s, intrepid travellers were visiting Niagara Falls, although Jasen suggested that by the 1820s, the romance had dulled with the circus atmosphere that soon ensued. Popular as it is today to decry the rampant commercialism of the attraction, with its brash casino and tawdry souvenir shops, similar complaints rose in the early years of tourism to the Falls. Perhaps the nadir was reached in 1827, when William Forsyth, a local hotelier, thought it the height of amusement to send a schooner full of "ferocious" animals over the Falls for the enjoyment of the local tourists — the animals were a rather tame collection, consisting of a buffalo, raccoons, a goose, a dog, and two small bears.[2] As Niagara Falls began to lose its wilderness image, the Thousand Islands in the St. Lawrence River, near Kingston, became a preferred destination, where picturesque voyageurs paddled the water and quaint cottages dotted the shoreline. However, just like Niagara Falls, the Thousand Islands was becoming more commercialized, and those wishing for a more rustic experience began to look north to Muskoka, where early settlement was just beginning. Tourists not only enjoyed the district's beautiful scenery, they could also take advantage of the benefits of Muskoka's clean, fresh air: in fact, physicians in the nineteenth century frequently prescribed a visit to the country as a panacea for any number of ailments. Fortunately, Muskoka was easily reached: the colonization roads, railways, and steamboats that were built to attract settlers made it easier for tourists (especially from Toronto) to arrive for their wilderness experience. There were already a few hotels in the major towns, but gradually canny settlers with waterfront properties realized that they could raise extra funds by encouraging tourists to lodge in their homes and by leading hunting and fishing expeditions.

As far back as 1861, James "Micky" McCabe and his wife were operating a tavern and inn in Gravenhurst, where weary travellers could expect a warm Irish welcome, according to Thomas McMurray. Another early hotel was William Cann's in Huntsville, the town's first, built in 1869. When Thomas Osborne arrived at Cann's hotel in May 1875 with his younger brother late at night to meet his very relieved father, he was especially taken with Mrs. Cann's (William Cann's sister-in-law, according to Osborne) warm welcome, and the hotel continued to be a port of call for Osborne in the years to come. One of the earliest "tourist" hotels was Rosseau House, built by an American, William H. Pratt, who located his grand resort near the village of Rosseau in 1870. W.E. Hamilton was much taken with the hotelier. Referring to him as "the inevitable Pratt," Hamilton described him as an "incorrigible joker," which had accordingly afforded Pratt some enemies in the district. But Hamilton enjoyed sitting with him at the hotel in the spring of 1875, smoking Havana cigars in the lounge.

Even Thomas McMurray, so focused on agricultural settlement in Muskoka, promoted tourism to the district as an adjunct to farming. In his 1871 guide, he included a letter from a Reverend Alex Kennedy of Pickering (he doesn't specify if this is Pickering, Ontario, or its namesake in Yorkshire), who wrote to McMurray in December 1870. "It has been my lot to see many corners of creation in several and distant lands; but, for romantic grandeur, I am not sure that I have seen anything to surpass Lake Muskoka, with its all but countless islands and its rocky and wooded shores. Without much hazard of prophetic failure, the day may be predicted, and not far distant either, when the wealthy in our large cities will erect villas for the summer residence of their families on the healthful and enchanting shores of Lake Muskoka."[3] Prophetic words, indeed.

One free grant settler who profited from the early tourist trade was Thomas Aitken, originally from the Shetland Islands, whose free grant land boasted Lake Rosseau waterfront, near the village of Windermere. Happily, the name Windermere would have conjured up visions of England's scenic Lake District, where Lake Windermere had long been a destination for artists and tourists. Aitken began to board tourists and sportsmen in his home in the early 1870s, and over the next few decades, he transformed his modest lodging house into Windermere House, a grand hotel that became a popular tourist destination. Other settlers were just as enterprising. Charles Minett arrived in Muskoka in 1869 as a free grant settler, with land also bordering Lake Rosseau, near the present village named after him. Upon building a frame house, he began to take in settlers as well as establishing a boat-building enterprise. Eventually his resort became Clevelands House, a business owned by his family until 1953. Gryffin Lodge on Mary Lake is an expansion of the boarding house that the Lawrence family ran after arriving in 1867. All three hotels remain in business to this day. More affordable were smaller tourist homes, which didn't necessarily have to have water frontage; they provided an opportunity for visitors to enjoy a modest vacation in the fresh air away from industrial centres such as Toronto.

Muskoka was also beginning to appeal to tourists from the United States. As the northern states were becoming industrialized and farmland had taken over the wilderness, Muskoka's accessibility led American tourists to the district, ready to enjoy a sportsman's paradise. In the August 22, 1875, edition of the *St. Louis Globe-Democrat*, an article by "Vidette" aptly described the charms of holidaying in Muskoka. Titled "Among the Trout Lakes and Romantic Woods of Canada: The Picturesque Wilds of the North Described: Glorious Sports for Hunters and Fishermen," the article outlined the journey to Muskoka and offered advice and information on the best places to hunt and fish. Muskoka was a destination "where there are very good summer hotels and accommodations of the best class, at from $1 to $1.50 per day.... Muskoka is much more attractive, as a summer resort, and cheaper than the Ottawa or St. Lawrence routes. [In Muskoka] visitors can dress as his tastes suggest and his pocket permits, and he is not ostracized if he have not a killing toilet.... This region that I have described affords new fields for tourists who have sickened of the humdrum life at the sea-side and watering places." A "killing toilet" is certainly requisite in many of the larger upscale hotels today, which are more "Toronto" than Muskoka with their spas and golf courses and fine dining. The Muskoka that Vidette described was comfortable, rustic, a place where one didn't have to put on airs.

The success of Muskoka's tourist industry was a testament to the resourcefulness of many of the settlers in the district who were able to turn their free grant into a thriving concern. And not only did some settlers benefit from tourism: entrepreneurs could see new possibilities, as well. The Northern Railway's early advertisements mainly focused on free grant settlers for business, but by the 1870s it was advertising tours into Muskoka, as well as lakes Simcoe, Couchiching, and Superior. One such excursion was advertised in the July 1, 1875, edition of the *Globe*. Tourists leaving Toronto were charged $5.50 for a round-trip fare to Bracebridge, $6 to Lake Rosseau, and $7 to Lake Joseph. And while A.P. Cockburn initially developed his steamboat service for free grant settlers, before long, he was offering package deals for tourists to visit Muskoka, the "popular and cheap summer resort." Perhaps the politicians and emigration adherents were relieved that there was finally an economic potential for free grant settlers who were otherwise unable to make a decent living. In fact, it is possible that had the early emigration agents recruited British hoteliers and innkeepers to Muskoka rather than farmers and the urban poor, the story of the free grants might have had quite a different outcome! And yet, tourism did not bring about prosperity to the entire region: wages for lower-level positions in the service industry are rarely lucrative. Unless settlers worked their way into ownership or management, most would be relegated to positions such as domestic- or labour-oriented jobs. As well, summer is relatively short in Muskoka: although there would be some tourists during the spring and fall, the majority of them would arrive in July and August, when the lakes were warm enough to swim in and the weather could be expected to be reasonable. Once the tourist season was over, those employed in the hotels would face a long winter with little employment.

The financial impact, however effective, was not the only change that tourism brought. The industry would change the social fabric of Muskoka, as well. As was pointed out in a previous chapter, in the early days of the free grant scheme, many settlers from Great Britain, for example, were pleased to find a less rigid class structure in Canada. Although society would have been socially stratified to some extent, with income and social positions being indicators of where one fit into the community, there were no lords or ladies, dukes or duchesses to contend with. Someone like Thomas McMurray, the son of a humble weaver, and a weaver himself for some time, gained a good deal of respect in the Muskoka district through his business and political influence. However, tourism changed this harmonious relationship in some ways, for wealthier tourists were unlikely to mingle with those who served them. Cottagers, as well, began to buy up waterfront properties, and they, too, formed their own friendships and associations, not always treating the "locals" with the respect they deserved. And so while many of the Muskoka settlers earned needed funds in a variety of ways — by working in the tourism industry; building cottages and resorts, docks, and boats; selling and delivering provisions to hotel guests and cottagers — those earning the minimum were unlikely to have enjoyed either the companionship of the cottagers or the hospitality offered by these new hotels and resorts.

As the district filled up, more non-British emigrants began to arrive, and these new settlers provided a sort of scapegoat for those who were still defending the free grants as an agricultural destination, despite negative reports. When it became apparent that the predominately British settlers were failing to succeed on their free grants, it was suggested that the solution lay in recruiting emigrants from what were regarded as less-genteel, or more rugged, countries. In 1873, a group of Icelanders arrived in Canada to escape poverty in their own country, led by twenty-two-year-old Sigtryggur Jonasson. They weren't the first Icelandic settlers to arrive in North America — a few decades ago, groups had already settled in parts of the United States. Now drawn to the free grant district in Muskoka, these new settlers set up a community six miles east of Rosseau, naming it Hekkla, after an active volcano in their homeland.[4] Their first winter was miserable: the temporary emigration shed the government provided proved to be inadequate against the cold, and provisions were low. And although emigration authorities believed that Icelanders would make good settlers, as they hailed from a wild, scrubby land with extreme weather conditions, the Icelanders would not be used to the dense foliage of Muskoka, and they would have had the same problems with rock and poor soil as other settlers. The following year, another group of Icelanders settled in Kinmount, near Lindsay in eastern Ontario, but they also suffered a good deal of hardship, including the deaths of several children, and they were no better off than their Muskoka counterparts. By 1875 many of these emigrants, from both

Kinmount and Hekkla, joined fellow countrymen in Manitoba and founded a community that eventually was named Gimli.

The Icelanders' experience as recounted here is, of course, a condensed version of what was at times a tragic story, but it follows a familiar pattern: settlers enticed from their homeland to farm unfamiliar terrain and Canadian officials doing little to help them. While many accounts of settlers' lives indicated that on the frontier, neighbours supported neighbours no matter what their country of origin, some rather distasteful comments were being expressed concerning the suitability of certain ethnic types for free grant farming. In the May 21, 1875, edition of the *Belfast News-Letter*, whose editorials and correspondents were often critical of Muskoka settlement, an editorial exemplified this attitude when it quoted Archibald McKellar. "In the *Orillia Packet* we observe a speech of Mr. McKellar, Immigration Minister, in which he says — 'Ontario had [*sic*] now no land left worth the attention of free-grant settlers ... and that while Muskoka, with its bad climate and poor soil, might do for dirty Swedes and Norwegians, the sons of Canadian farmers would not look at it.'" Even during the early debates on the free grant scheme in 1868, McKellar voiced his reservations, which was perhaps to his credit, as he was brave enough to suggest Muskoka may not be able to sustain a large agricultural community. But his assumption that the land was only fit for "dirty" foreigners was unpalatable, to say the least, even giving him some leeway as he may have simply been voicing the commonly held sentiments of that period in history. However, the *Belfast-Newsletter* wasn't cutting him any slack: it editorialized that presumably the Irish were equally held in such low regard. For decades, the Irish had borne the brunt of such attitudes in their experience settling in North America, and it stands to reason that the *Belfast-Newsletter* would be unlikely to tolerate statements such as McKellar's.

McKellar's contention that Canadian farmers wouldn't look at the free grants was wrong, as well. Farmers who couldn't afford land in the more settled districts of southern Ontario did, in fact, attempt to farm in Muskoka. But if their free grant failed to prosper, many would have had the option of returning to family in their hometowns or to other centres in the south where they could look for employment opportunities other than farming. Impoverished settlers far from home would have fewer options. At any rate,

McKellar did little to address the plight of settlers who weren't "dirty" foreigners or Canadian. What of the British emigrants — presumably ones
he didn't regard as "dirty" — who had already been lured to Muskoka
and were struggling to survive? Their options were just as limited as the
Icelanders'. Perhaps it was just too painful to contemplate those settlers' destinies. Interestingly, McKellar's views on who was best suited for Muskoka
settlement were echoed by John Clay, the writer who had rhapsodized over
his travels along Muskoka waterways. Clay noted that the dramatic rock
formations might attract tourists, but were useless for farmers. Observing
that southern Ontario was a "garden" compared to Muskoka, he described
the hard life the settlers endured. He observed, "For English or Scotchmen
it will not suit. Irishmen may thrive better; but the men to succeed there
are Norwegians, Icelanders, and such like — people who have come from
a poor district and been accustomed to a simple and frugal style of living.
Such a class of immigrants the Canadian Government are wisely encouraging to settle."[5] Neither McKellar nor Clay explained how anyone, however
accustomed to poverty and a rugged terrain, could manage to sow crops in
poor soil or on rocky outcrops. Most disturbing was the suggestion, albeit
veiled to some degree, that these "lesser" races were people who were all
brawn but no brain, and perhaps regarded as too ignorant to notice that
Muskoka held little fertile land.

⪚

In March and April 1874, a two-part article by Harriet Barbara King
was published in *Atlantic Monthly*, the venerable Boston-based magazine, whose contributors included Henry Wadsworth Longfellow, Ralph
Waldo Emerson, and Harriet Beecher Stowe. As a relatively obscure free
grant settler, King must have been quite honoured to be on the same
roster as those distinguished writers. Her article was titled "Life in the
Backwoods of Canada," and in it, she described her family's experience
on the free grant lands. She didn't hesitate to report on the hardships and
privations of Muskoka settlement. The impact of these articles might have
been slight: the contents of magazines are often quickly forgotten, soon
to be replaced by a new edition. But in 1878, King compiled these articles
anonymously in her *Letters from Muskoka by an Emigrant Lady*, under the
imprint of Richard Bentley and Son, a prominent publisher in London,

England, who had published Susanna Moodie's *Roughing It in the Bush* back in 1852. A book has a much longer shelf life than a magazine, and this time her observations definitely made their way to England. As we have seen, King was very direct in her opinion of Muskoka. "It is needless to say to those who know anything of Muskoka, that the misgivings were fully realised, and the hopes proved mere delusions, and melted away imperceptibly as those airy fabrics often do. We were certainly much deceived by the accounts given of Muskoka; after a four years' residence I am inclined to think that from the very first the capabilities of its soil for agricultural purposes have been greatly exaggerated."[6] Oddly, she softened her approach to the free grants in two articles that she tacked on at the end of the book: "Terra Incognita, or, the Wilds of Muskoka" and "A Plea for Poor Emigrants," the latter of which was published in the *Free Grants Gazette*. In "Terra Incognita" she chastised Arthur Clayden, whom she didn't name but identified as the writer who contributed information about Muskoka in the *Daily News*. She charged that he "most unduly disparaged the little town of Bracebridge," and as he had visited during the rainy season only for a few days, "his opinion can hardly be received as gospel truth."[7] She went on to assure her readers that hard-working settlers should see success, and only "black sheeps [*sic*]" would fail. The discrepancies between these articles and the main story are confusing; nevertheless, her vivid description of the hardships in Muskoka, coupled with her obvious despair, suggests that there was some truth to her tale. The London *Times* featured a review of her book on June 12, 1878:

[*Letters from Muskoka* is a] half-plaintive, half good-humoured story of the trials and struggles of an English lady in attempting to adapt herself to the rough conditions of a settler's life in the Canadian bush.... From first to last the letters are full of mishaps, disappointments, and failure, borne, on the whole, with cheerfulness.... The moral evidently is that neither Muskoka nor any other new emigrant ground is suited to fine ladies and gentlemen without capital and without adaptability. The story of the Emigrant Lady is decidedly interesting and simply told, and it is perhaps well that intending emigrants should know the dark side of a picture which is almost invariably coloured with the brightest rose tints.

Whether or not King fictionalized her memoir, as some believe, is unimportant. An experienced settler, she had more credibility than those who wrote glowing accounts of Muskoka with the aim to make political or economic gains.

∾

The "losers" of this chapter were generally silent and depended on the reports of others to voice their despair. On February 28, 1878, ten years to the day since the Free Grants Act was passed, the *Bristol Mercury and Post* published a letter from "An Englishman in Canada," who wrote about Muskoka's many deficiencies. He described a family whom he had visited in Chaffey Township:

> I know families barely able to scratch an existence from the hungry soil, and whose daily thought is — what shall we eat to-morrow, and what are things to come to? I once came on a small clearing in June, miles from others, and found a woman with four children with nothing what-ever in the house but a few potatoes — no milk, no flour, no fatness of any kind — the father had gone out walking 25 miles to get provisions! [He] could not possibly return in as many hours. *The children were in bed at mid-day as the best refuge from the mosquitoes.*

Frederick de la Fosse, whose observations on pioneering were discussed in chapter four, described even worse examples of poverty. He wrote his account many years after his sojourn in Muskoka, which began in 1878, so his observations were made around the same time as those made by the "Englishman in Canada." He had no hidden agenda in the telling of his tale, for he had nothing to gain by exaggerating the poverty he encountered in the backwoods. De la Fosse was a keen observer as he travelled about the district as a young man. His descriptions of destitute homesteaders are poignant, and provide a voice for those who had little opportunity to speak for themselves. He encountered a couple near Utterson, living in a run-down shanty, with newspapers plastered across the window openings and a pair of boots serving as door hinges. He was appalled by their poverty:

> This sordid style of living was somewhat of a surprise, but it was nothing to the shock I received when, in answer to my timid knock, a deep female voice called out fiercely. "What are you wanting?" ... The door was thrown open suddenly by a middle-aged woman of massive build and menacing aspect.... The upper part of her clothing consisted of a torn blouse, exhibiting more of her bust than was generally considered essential in society in those days, and the lower half was encased in a ragged pair of trousers. Her dishevelled hair hung partly down her back and partly over her face.... I followed her into the shack.... The furniture was home-made and meagre in the extreme.... It was not difficult for me to realize how fierce [their] battle had been.[8]

In a later trek through the woods, de la Fosse observed another family living in desperate conditions in the vicinity of Buck Lake:

> Poverty had rendered them careless and even desperate. There were six of them, father and mother, two sons and two daughters. The filth of the interior of their domicile was indescribable. One or two of them, through drinking snow water, had contracted goitre and were not very presentable-looking beings. The girls, grown to womanhood, were in a partially demented condition. They had lived such lives of horror that they fled at the approach of a human being and would hide themselves in corners of the fence or flee into the woods or cower in the pig-sty. Theirs was not an isolated case.[9]

Fosse's contention that there were other families in such distress shows us that poverty was not uncommon in the district. The hard physical labour, the long, cold winters, a poor diet, and the district's isolation would all have contributed to the terrible conditions in which they were living.

~

In 1879, one of Muskoka's leading figures made a sudden and permanent departure. After an eighteen-year residence in Muskoka, Thomas McMurray, who had built a modest business empire and served as a reeve and Crown land agent, sold the Parry Sound *North Star* in March 1879 and resigned from his post as Crown land agent three months later. He moved to Toronto's Parkdale neighbourhood and resumed his temperance activities, travelling about the country and lecturing on the subject that had captivated him since he was a teenager. His newspaper businesses had suffered, as there was fierce competition with rival papers, the *Free Grant Gazette* and the *Muskoka Herald*. Despite the poverty de la Fosse encountered in Muskoka, commercial enterprises, as well as the tourist industry, were blossoming in the district, and the romance and excitement of those early days when McMurray was one of the district's first pioneers had perhaps begun to wane. He had come a long way since he and his family had camped out in their roofless home in 1861, savouring the thrill of living rough in the backwoods. We do know that McMurray was a man who frequently reinvented himself — perhaps he was repeating a pattern of a lifetime. And yet, there is a finality about his leaving that leaves one pondering about his departure. McMurray was a resourceful man and must be credited for his contribution to Muskoka's many success stories, but the district had failed to become the successful agricultural destination he had predicted. Not surprisingly, he chose this time to follow other interests.

~

From the mid-1870s to the early 1880s, detailed atlases of communities across Canada were published. They were wonderful compendiums of historical information, with descriptions of communities, illustrations, and detailed maps of both rural and urban areas. The atlases were intended to not just inform their readers but to showcase the various districts. In 1879, the Toronto publishing firm H.R. Page produced the *Guide Book & Atlas of*

Muskoka and Parry Sound Districts, with a forty-three-page introduction by W.E. Hamilton, who lived in Bracebridge between 1875 and 1879. He was yet another one of the memorable characters who incongruously appeared in the Muskoka backwoods, rather like Colonel Maude with his lavish entertaining and British-style hunting parties in the bush. A graduate of Trinity College in Dublin, Hamilton was described by James Boyer as "a fine scholar and a genial soul, although rather absent-minded and eccentric.... He had a penchant for making writing paper and envelopes, also shirt collars and cuffs, from the inner bark of the birch tree, a custom which had gone out of fashion, even in Muskoka."[10] In a memoir published in 1895, Hamilton admitted to his boyhood exploits — he received his share of canings for his shenanigans — and briefly mentioned his early travels to Paris, Belgium, Cologne, the West Indies, and South and Central America, as well as to the United States and Canada. He readily acknowledged his eccentric behaviour. While living in a house in Bracebridge, he had been given a snowy owl by a "lady friend," and he confided, "The huge bird would fly across the room, dodging books and tea-cups without making the least sound."[11] One night the owl nearly strangled him when it landed on his bed; he wakened to see its huge talons hovering near his neck. Anthony McGill, a schoolmaster in Bracebridge, reported that at one point, Hamilton "nested" in rooms above the *Free Grant Gazette* office, and although an experienced traveller and a deep thinker, "he had become so dependent on the cup that cheers but also inebriates, as to make prolonged mental excursions distinctly fatiguing."[12] McGill certainly excelled at creative euphemism!

Hamilton provided a comprehensive history and description of the community, an overview of businesses, hotels, churches, and the like, with a handy business directory at the end of the book. The handsome lithographs of the district's settlements and natural landscape were provided by Seymour Penson, giving the reader an almost photographic view of Muskoka's early days. Most important, despite the growing criticism of Muskoka in the press, Hamilton was able to turn the atlas into an opportunity to put the district in a favourable light. He may, however, have gotten a little carried away. Using statistics and questionable arithmetic, he suggested that Muskoka's future as a settlement knew no bounds. In the introduction, he advised readers that the free grant district was "in round numbers, five times as large as either the Province of

Prince Edward's [sic] Island in our Dominion, or Delaware in the United States; five times the size of Connecticut; one-fifth larger than New Jersey or Massachusett [sic]; within one-eleventh of the size of Belgium; lacking a sixth of the extent of Holland; and a third of that of Denmark or Switzerland."[13] Consequently, he calculated that "Taking the limited extremes of density of population among the nations, states and provinces above cited ... our free grant districts could sustain 460,000 people judged by the standard of Prince Edward's Island, or 4,400,000 judged by that of Belgium."[14] *Four and a half million people?* In fairness, he backtracked a little, suggesting that an earlier estimate he had made that perhaps one hundred thousand people, eighty percent of whom would be employed in agriculture, with the remainder in commerce, manufacturing, and other such pursuits, was a more realistic calculation for Muskoka's potential population. Having assured readers that the district could sustain a growing number of settlers, he bravely tackled that touchy Muskoka subject: rock. And he did this with aplomb. "Now, gentle reader, I must bring you to something on which all the abusive epithets in the English language have been poured out in lavish abundance, a hard, rugged, undeniable fact — the Muskoka rock.... These rocky barriers, which fringe our territory and frown on the incomer, are *not* true samples of Muskoka land."[15] The word *fringe* echoes McMurray's and others' reassurances that interior land, behind the district's roads, was virtually rock-free and fertile. This was a convenient way to entice settlement — suggesting what the eye *couldn't* see was prime agricultural land. However, the reality was that the ancient rock did not spontaneously appear where surveyors laid out roads; it was distributed throughout the bush, sometimes far from a spectator's view. And yet, Hamilton confided, even when a settler's land *was* rocky, still there was hope, it seemed. He extolled the rock's qualities of heat retention, as well as its nourishing qualities for soil, which could be attributed to "a weathering of the feldsphathic portion, which yields comminuted plant-food in a very available form."[16] It is doubtful if words such as *feldsphathic* and *comminuted* would have reassured a settler who was flummoxed by his rock's inability to grow crops.

Perhaps the most compelling, and poignant, feature of the atlas are the maps of each township of Muskoka. These delineated each free grant lot, labelled with the name of the settler who had claimed it. Some townships, such as Draper, Macaulay, Watt, and Stephenson, were heavily settled. Other maps show another story. Machar Township, roughly halfway between Huntsville and North Bay, had no settlers, perhaps because it was simply too far north. Wood Township, which lies on the western shore of Lake Muskoka, east of Gravenhurst, had only a few settlers near the shoreline. Even Hamilton admitted that most of Wood was rocky; in fact, today, the Torrance Barrens Dark Sky Reserve is located in the township. Because the area is virtually unpopulated even now, there are few artificial lights, allowing visitors a clear view of the night sky. For some odd reason, the atlas revealed that a Jno (John) Drummond settled smack in the middle of the empty township. He might have been a hermit who simply preferred to live far from his neighbours, or he could have annoyed a land agent with a predilection for practical jokes.

The early maps are a testament to the high hopes of the early free grant adherents: the population predictions made by Hamilton almost seem reasonable with such dense settlement in so many townships. And yet, there's no way to tell if all the names carefully recorded on each lot represented settlers who were still farming in the district. In *Letters from Muskoka*, Mrs. King suggested that she left her free grant lot in 1875, but her name remained on the Stephenson Township map in 1879. It's reasonable to assume that many settlers, those on poor land especially, might have already left their lot at the time of publication. The emptiness of Muskoka's back roads today attests to the fact that thousands of settlers must have abandoned what was once their dream of a prosperous future. Hamilton's atlas was perhaps the last concerted effort to draw settlers to Muskoka. While the government continued to publish information guides on free grant lands for aspiring emigrants during the next decade, Muskoka began to take a back seat to the more fertile Nipissing District to the north.

Chapter Eight

Days of Reckoning

The general effect of the Free Grant policy has therefore been to people Muskoka, but to people it to a great extent in the way least likely to show early large results.[1]
— *Report of the Commissioners,*
Ontario Agricultural Commission

Twelve years after the Free Grants Act was passed, following years of attacks on the settlement scheme in the press, the government's long silence was suddenly broken. In June 1880, the members of the Ontario Agricultural Commission announced that over the past years, the older, settled parts of the province had received the lion's share of their attention, and it was time to visit the "newer and outlying" sections — particularly Muskoka and Parry Sound. The distinction of the district's free grant status did not go unnoticed. "Having regard to the circumstances generally under which the electoral district of Muskoka and Parry Sound had been settled, it was thought most expedient that some members of the Commission should make a personal visit to that district."[2] The announcement was quite restrained: it didn't explain *why* it was "most expedient" that the investigation be made. Nevertheless, the commissioners had made it clear that Muskoka and Parry Sound's free grant status set the district apart from the conventionally settled districts of southern Ontario. And it could be that the accumulation of criticism over the free grant scheme had forced the commission's hand.

On August 24, 1880, the commission sent three investigators to Muskoka on a fact-finding exercise to assess the progress free grant settlers had made since the scheme had been initiated twelve years before. William Brown, Edward Stock, and A.H. Dymond, accompanied by George Eyvel, a shorthand writer, left Toronto in the morning and arrived in Bracebridge at 3:00 p.m. Over the next eleven days, they managed to hold nine sittings, to speak to fifty "witnesses" (Muskoka farmers), and to visit twenty-seven townships. It isn't clear how these witnesses were chosen — such information would have been helpful, as more successful farmers would give a rosier report than ones who were failing. The commissioners claimed that none of the farmers asked for or were given any recompense, and many had travelled several miles on foot to appear before them. The lengthy testimonies given by these farmers reveal that many seemed to have had some measure of success with their Muskoka farms. According to the subsequent report, the sessions were "informal and conversational," and there was no coercion when they gave their testimony. One thing is for sure: these commissioners were dedicated to their task. One hour after their arrival in Bracebridge, they commenced the first session, which lasted well into the late evening.

A *Globe* correspondent had joined the proceedings as the commissioners met with farmers from all over Muskoka. In a September 11, 1880, editorial, the paper praised the "plain, unvarnished statements" of the farmers, a welcome change from the overblown guides written about Muskoka thus far. "Descriptive pamphlets, no matter how moderately worded, are always open to the suspicion of being pitched in too high a key." But when confronted with evidence of hardship in the district, yet again, the editorial repeated the tired refrain that many settlers had chosen poor land, had failed to rotate crops and hadn't cleared enough land in the first place. The sternest lectures that admonished Muskoka settlers for their ineptness as farmers always seemed to come from non-Muskokan sources. How frustrating that must have been for those who were actually living the experience.

The testimonies of the witnesses only told part of the story, however. The subsequent report was published the following year as Appendix R in the Ontario Agricultural Commission's *Report of the Commissioners*. This almost-six-hundred-page book was a compilation of reports from an army of commissioners who had travelled throughout the province to report on general aspects of farming, including crops, forestry, livestock, dairy farming, bee-keeping, orchards, as well as agricultural bookkeeping and labour considerations. Only one section focused on specific regions of Ontario — Muskoka and Parry Sound, followed by Manitoulin and Sault Ste. Marie. The section on Muskoka was a detailed consideration of the commissioners' findings on their visit to the district in 1880.[3]

The commissioners' final report not only contained the witnesses' testimonies, but the commissioners' personal observations of the district, as well. Some roads were in excellent condition, they noted, but many were not, and they felt improvements would likely be completed as more municipal incorporations were formed in the district; presumably the local towns could then be held responsible for the costs and not the province. It is doubtful, however, that a district as underpopulated as Muskoka would have the necessary funds to support such infrastructure. The commissioners described the "rugged and broken" land, but they added that this picturesque landscape, when bordered by lakes, would especially appeal to tourists. They reported that northerly regions of Muskoka were quite fertile, although they failed to specify where in Muskoka these regions were. Thus far, all seemed fairly benign: the settlers seemed content on the whole. But the commissioners obviously saw beyond the settlers' testimonies: they witnessed a good deal of poverty that other visiting dignitaries seemed to have missed over the years. Referring to the Free Grants and Homestead Act, they wrote:

> This legislation, while it has had the effect of attracting to the District a population now estimated at about 30,000 souls, naturally invited in the first instance the class of persons who were the least likely to give signs of rapid progress. One of the witnesses who described his means upon entering upon his location as "exactly fourteen pence, a little pork and flour, a wife and six children," was a representative man in this sense. When it is considered that even in more favoured regions the seasons will not always befriend the husbandman, the wonder is that so much has been accomplished.[4]

These words were cleverly written: without exactly pointing fingers, they pinpointed the major weakness of the Free Grants Act — settling poor people on poor land had been inadvisable. Were Styleman Herring's emigration club members, and others like them, among "the class of persons who were the least likely to give signs of rapid progress"? Despite their careful words, it is obvious that the commissioners found the free grant policy to be flawed. Doubts had been expressed in the Legislature as early as 1868, but the free grant advocates hadn't listened. Now the result of such faulty judgement was clear: despite the small pockets of fertile land, probably the areas where "much has been accomplished," Muskoka should never have been designated as a purely agricultural destination for emigrants or any other settlers.

The commissioners went on to note that the clearings settlers had made were still small in comparison to the land they held, and in fact, clearance was often either deferred indefinitely or had ceased altogether, which leads one to assume that many settlers had either fled their farm or simply given up attempts to clear it. And yet, just as the commissioners obliquely placed the blame on those who devised the free grant scheme, they delivered this cryptic message: "The general effect of the Free Grant policy has therefore been to people Muskoka, but to people it to a great extent in the way least likely to show early large results. The causes of individual success or failure have been found, however, more frequently in the man than in the circumstances.... The whole thing generally turns on the settler's adaptability to the life he has chosen."[5] On one hand, the very *nature* of the free grant scheme had led to settlers' misfortunes; on the other, if a settler had "adapted" to his circumstances, he might be successful. The commissioners didn't explain exactly how a settler should adapt to his land, only noted that men who were "frugal, industrious, persistent, and courageous" had the best chance of success. However, by suggesting that the settlers themselves were basically the ones who set their own destiny, the commissioners showed that they couldn't seem to decide whether their failure was due to moral weaknesses, or due to the settlers' lack of agricultural knowledge and prior experience, as well as the infertility of their land.

The final report noted that "A large proportion of the settlers have been, as may be supposed, persons without means, or with very limited means indeed.... The country is densely wooded; consequently, every foot of cultivable ground has had to be cleared with the axe; and, but for the lumbering industry ... not a few of the settlers would have found subsistence impossible. Having regard in fact to the nature of the country, and the class to which the majority of the settlers belong, the progress made has been not only satisfactory, but even, in some respects, surprising."[6] But despite some progress, the three commissioners pointed out that "[i]n Muskoka the stumps still dot the ground, manure is scarcely applied, drainage is particularly unknown, and, from the first operation of breaking up the soil to the final harvesting of the crop, many of the simplest essentials to success are wanting."[7] This begs the question: what would many of those emigrants, most particularly the ones from London's East End, have known about fertilizers, drainage, or harvesting? The commissioners felt that with "proper management of the land," the settlers might be successful if they could at least grow enough wheat for their own consumption, but this would leave them little profit margin. The final report suggested that men of some means were successful in the district, who "have thus infused a spirit of progress and energy into its somewhat primitive style of agriculture, and a very fair representation of improved stock is to be found in many places."[8] Men like the enterprising Colonel Maude probably fell into this category, but those with capital and good land could hardly be expected to turn around the prospects of poorer settlers on unfit land.

Desperate to find some good news for Muskoka, the final report suggested that butter- and cheese-making might be profitable, but cooperative associations would be difficult to organize because of the "comparative" sparseness of the population and difficult communications in the district. The conclusion made by the commentary on the commissioners' findings was succinct: "Looking at the capacity of the district from a purely agricultural point of view, and leaving entirely out of consideration all those questions of policy connected with the Free Grant system which apply thereto, the visiting Commissioners appear to have come to the conclusion that, as a stock-rearing and sheep-farming region, the District of Muskoka must in the future chiefly be regarded."[9] Sheep farming was, indeed, a lucrative enterprise for Muskoka farmers for some years. Muskoka lamb graced the tables at the growing number of hotels in the district, and the sheep's wool could be sold — frequently to the Bird Woollen Mills, which was founded in 1872 and situated on the north side of Bracebridge Falls. However, stock rearing and sheep farming gradually diminished in popularity over the years. Predators such as wolves and coyotes were a threat to livestock, and as transport improved throughout the district, cheaper wool and cheaper meat could be brought in from the outside. Farmers' wives who had previously spun and woven the wool for the mill to earn extra cash may have lamented the loss of income, but sheep farming never flourished as the commissioners had hoped.

Despite their attempt to take a positive attitude about Muskoka and refrain from blatantly placing blame, the commissioners had identified the true culprits behind the scheme: those who set the initial policy. However, it was one thing to indentify the problem, quite another to do something about it.

~

As has happened often in this story, just as one source leads us to one conclusion, another seems to refute it. Despite the obvious hardships that the commissioners reported on during their investigation of Muskoka farming, another report suggested quite the opposite. In his 1884 memoir, *Muskoka Sketch*, W.E. Hamilton described his huge effort to enter Muskoka into the provincial agricultural exhibition in Hamilton, Ontario, in 1880. Although James Boyer had described a similar entry in an exhibition in Toronto back in the early 1870s, Hamilton wrote as if this was a new initiative. With the exhibition less than two weeks away, he scrambled to find produce from local farms to display, and in his haste, bypassed the Muskoka Agricultural Society, claiming there simply wasn't time for it to organize such a task. He and J.W. Dill, a Bracebridge shopkeeper, visited farms within a six-mile radius of Bracebridge, collecting soil samples, wood samples, specimens of iron, and, of course, local produce. Frederick de la Fosse's mentor, Captain Harston, whose agricultural skills de la Fosse expressed doubts about, donated a selection of millet and other grains. Hamilton enthused that Muskoka's forty-by-twelve-foot table was loaded with splendid apples, grapes, radishes, corn, onions, and potatoes. The latter, he reported, were "grown on a flat Bracebridge rock, artificially covered with soil, by a canny Scotsman from Aberdeen, who thus utilized the heat-giving qualities of the stone to force a crop."[10]

Perhaps Hamilton wasn't exaggerating in his atlas, published the year before, about the fertility of Muskoka rock! The exhibit received a special diploma from the exhibition authorities. The final page of *Muskoka Sketch* contained a review of an advanced copy of the book by the *Hamilton Spectator*, dated December 31, 1883. In it, the reviewer suggested that the provincial government never funded the exhibit that Hamilton had so diligently organized, but did fund a following one in Toronto. Apparently, the government had "frowned upon" a provincial exhibition being held in Hamilton, rather than the province's capital.

What remains clear from Hamilton's exhibition is that a good portion of the Bracebridge area was fertile, and, therefore, it is not surprising he was so successful. The enterprise didn't refute the commissioners' findings, it just emphasized that Muskoka farms could prosper, but mainly in areas with good soil and little rock.

~

Emigration to the colonies remained a key issue in Britain, and our old friend Styleman Herring was still very much involved in efforts to encourage emigration. On March 22, 1881, he was one in a series of speakers to address the Royal Colonial Institute in London, following an address by the reformer William McCullagh Torrens, a Liberal MP, lobbyist, and cofounder of the National Emigration League and of the Clerkenwell Emigration Society. In his address, Herring stated, "… I feel myself that God has given us the English Colonies throughout the world to people, and that it is our national duty in every way to promote emigration."[11] The Aboriginal populations in the lands that God had (apparently) happily handed over to Britain, lands that they most rightly would have considered to be their own, might have taken issue with this rather facetious comment, but Herring was merely expressing a sentiment that was commonplace in colonial Victorian society. Along with other contributors to the proceedings that day, he was firm in the belief that emigration would solve Britain's problems with unemployment and poverty, and that Britain had a God-given right to colonize land they really had no legitimate claim to.

As in 1874, when Herring claimed to have lost confidence in Canada as a destination for his society's emigrants, he explained why he had made that decision: "We all know that Canada has not reaped so much advantage as was expected in helping emigrants, because in a great many instances directly they got over to the Dominion they secured free railway tickets to Detroit, and the Yankees got the benefit of it, while the Canadian Government was very much offended."[12] He believed that many of the farmers had failed because they neglected to adapt to their new circumstances. "Our Society has also sent out a good many of the middle-class, and a still larger number of the humbler classes, and we find that a great many of them, when they get there, have to unlearn English farming, &c., before they can learn the Colonial systems." It would be best, he added, that emigrants drop their "pride in English ways."[13] This was rather a low blow, uncharacteristic of Herring. Unlike the commissioners, who cited the Muskoka farmers' ignorance rather than their pride, Herring refused to recognize the obvious — the farmers could hardly be blamed for their own lack of experience in Canadian agricultural methods, especially if they came from Britain's cities or towns. Not only did British farmers have to adapt to Canadian practices, but urban dwellers had to begin from square one. There is a subtle hint that Herring was still smarting from his visit to Muskoka back in 1870, when he and Charles Marshall were paraded throughout the free grant district and assured that all was well. It wouldn't do to accuse those dignitaries that they had been less than truthful about the suitability of the free grant lands for agriculture: it was much easier to blame the settlers themselves.

During his speech to the institute, he touched briefly on land grants. "I am not saying anything about the land offered by the Colonies, I think it better not; neither would I recommend any man going out straight from England to settle at once on any of the land so offered."[14] This was quite a departure from his early belief that the Free Grants Act would be an "immense boon" for his poor parishioners. His words *I think it better not* speak volumes, for either he felt he had said enough already by supporting the free grant scheme, which had come under attack over the years, or he didn't trust himself not to blame the Canadian proponents who had devised the scheme. It wouldn't do, however, in such august company of the Royal Colonial Institute, to denigrate the government of one of their colonies, and so Herring kept his silence. Before long, he was to visit Canada once again; there was no point in alienating his future hosts.

~

In January 1882, the *Globe* published a three-part feature on Muskoka penned by a special correspondent. The author had travelled throughout the district to assess how the settlers were faring after devastating bush fires had spread across a dozen townships the previous autumn. Disguising himself alternately as a lumberman or labourer, he tramped across the district, knocking on doors and asking for meals, thus gaining the trust of the settlers, who were candid about their troubles. He observed that fires in any district of Ontario would cause considerable hardship, but the Muskoka settlers were already so poor that it was difficult for them to recover from the widespread destruction. The combination of the aftermath of the fires and the poverty he encountered fuelled his observations. On January 7, 1882, he wrote: "A more desolate region could scarcely exist in Ontario. It is a perfect wilderness of rocks, blackened trees, and prostrate and charred timbers and coal and ashes." He observed huge boulders in fields; one Muskoka resident joked that had such boulders appeared in the western prairies, a hotel would immediately be erected to attract tourists!

As his journey progressed, he described one- and two-room log shanties with low ceilings, tiny windows, all of them set far apart and all but inaccessible. Many settlers who had already scarce supplies lost not only their homes, but clothing, bedding, stoves, and fireplaces in the bush fires, resulting in an inability to stay warm. Some were reduced to living off flour and potatoes. As he visited the farmers, he found that many were too proud to ask for handouts, and were too poor to risk taking out mortgages on their properties. Some local aid was available, however. The reeves of the Muskoka townships had formed a Central Relief Committee, based in Bracebridge, and they appealed both within Muskoka and throughout Ontario for funds. How successful this plea was is not immediately evident, but it did spark this rather half-hearted response in London, Ontario, from what seemed to be a budget committee for city council. The London *Advertiser* reported the proceedings on October 29, 1881, a few months prior to the *Globe*'s report. The committee had received a letter from the reeve in Bracebridge, explaining that $30,000 was needed by Muskokans who had suffered losses in the recent fires. After the letter was read out, this curious exchange between the aldermen took place:

Ald. Jones — Well, we have been ready to assist our neighbors over the lines, and I should think we ought to aid our own countrymen.

Ald. Cowan — Well, unless we think the Council would pass it there is no use of making a motion.

Ald. Jones — Oh give them $100.

Ald. Pritchard — I think the Government should take hold of such cases as this.

Ald. Raynor — When did this fire occur?

Ald. Cowan — During the months of August and September.

Ald. Jones — I move we grant $50.

Ald. Pritchard — I second that.

The committee decided to lay the matter over till proper enquiries could be made into the merits of the case.

Even had the London committee members roused themselves to be a little more generous — or to send money at all — it was difficult for the relief committee to find settlers who needed help in the far-flung reaches of the district, and many, the *Globe* correspondent noted, went without any aid at all. Still, he ended on a positive note, suggesting that some settlers were successful with stock rearing, and many had been able to procure jobs in the lumbering trade.

Naturally, those legislators who supported the free grants could not be held responsible for natural disasters in Muskoka. (As usual, the settlers themselves were blamed for carelessly torching their land in order to clear it during a prolonged drought.) Clearly, however, the fires exacerbated the settlers' already desperate situation — those who had little income would find it all the harder to recoup losses suffered by the fire. Settlers located on inaccessible and remote locations were left on their own to rebuild houses and to procure household goods lost in the flames. I have found no report of relief organized by the federal or provincial governments, although it may have been given. If relief efforts were solely a municipal responsibility, it was an inadequate response, to say the least.

~

The opening up of Manitoba for settlement could have been the catalyst that sparked Styleman Herring's second visit to Canada in 1882. Herring set out on June 28 from Liverpool with a party of two hundred emigrants — half of whom were orphans — on board the *Parisian*. He was accompanied by John James Jones, a London school board member and a director of the London Samaritan Society. The *Globe* ran a front-page article about Herring and Jones's visit on July 14, 1882, explaining that over the past fourteen years, Herring had sent out forty-five hundred emigrants to Canada and now wanted to see how they were faring. Herring's two-month-long trip was ambitious: according to reports, he was in Canada for sixteen weeks, travelled fifteen hundred miles, and not only traversed Ontario, including Muskoka, but also landed in Winnipeg, presumably to scout out possibilities for his emigrants there.

Unfortunately, we don't have as detailed a description of Herring's 1882 visit such as the one provided by Charles Marshall in 1870. The *Globe* reported that he preached at Toronto's St. James Cathedral on September 14, although the present-day archivist at St. James found no reference to this occasion as few records exist from this period. However, a diocesan archivist she consulted found a document that listed Herring as a preacher at All Saints Church, at the corner of Dundas and Sherbourne Streets, on the same date. *Nearly Forty Years*, Herring's biography, included a brief description of Herring's visit. "I am glad to say that none could have been more handsomely treated than Mr. Herring was by Canadian friends. He was fêted, lionised, and even entertained by the then Prime Minister, Sir John A. Macdonald; was shown over Niagara; slept on the same bed that the Duke of Connaught slept on when he visited Hamilton; and was, altogether, treated most hospitably."[15]

In twelve years, Herring had come a long way — from a rustic banquet with the premier of Ontario in a modest Bracebridge hotel to a much grander meeting with the prime minister of Canada. Of course, he already hobnobbed with aristocracy back in London, but to be "lionised" in this fashion must have confirmed that his work in Canada had been regarded as a success. There is no doubt that Herring was an honourable man: he could have inherited his father's comfortable parish in the lovely village of

Thorpe; instead, he sacrificed his life working in the overcrowded streets of Clerkenwell. After years of public service, he deserved the hearty welcome (and sightseeing tour) from his Canadian hosts. If he had any qualms over his role in encouraging free grant settlement, he failed to address the issue directly. Of course, it is possible on his second visit to Muskoka in September 1882, his hosts had again carefully micromanaged his trip through the woods. What is clear is that his letters to the editor of the *Times* had certainly dwindled at this juncture — there were no further endorsements, let alone criticism, of the free grant lands after his initial enthusiasm in the early 1870s. Perhaps Herring's endorsement for Manitoba as a destination for his emigrants helped him reconcile his past efforts. Now that he had turned his attention away from the free grant lands in Muskoka, he was repeating the entire exercise of sending settlers to a part of Canada he likely knew little about. By now, the CPR was recruiting emigrants to help build the railway into the Northwest, and both farming and labouring jobs in Manitoba were seen as good opportunities by emigration agents in Britain. In a *Winnipeg Times* report on emigration published January 22, 1883, a letter from Herring was included; in it, he assured readers that he was sending emigrants to the northwest that year. The *Winnipeg Times* reported that Herring had recently addressed the Royal Colonial Institute, and a summary of his speech had been published widely in the press. With his customary confidence, Herring had confided, "I think we Englishmen have first of all to thank God that in Manitoba at the present moment they can grow the very finest wheat that is to be found, I believe, in the whole world.... I have no hesitation in recommending Manitoba most warmly.... I can honestly say that if those whom I saw or heard of (certainly the majority) had remained in England, they would not have been in anything like the same good position that they are now." Did Herring know anything of prairie droughts, of locust plagues, severe winter and summer weather? Had he considered the isolation of farming the vast prairies, a hugely different experience compared to Muskoka settlement, where one could at least reach a major city such as Toronto in a matter of hours. And how did he know that Manitoba wheat was the *world's* finest? It may well have been, but he could hardly have known that at the time. Yet again, Herring's enthusiasm overrode common sense, for, as with the free grant scheme in Muskoka, he again naively believed his hosts' assurances without question.

~

Emigration became a contentious issue within Ontario's trade union community, which had its roots in the first half of the nineteenth century, when small societies, representing various trades, banded together to provide mutual support for members in times of need, brought on by unemployment, illness, or other misfortunes. As the decades wore on and industrialization made inroads into Canada, these societies became more organized. In 1873, the Canadian Labour Union was created, although initially its members all hailed from Ontario, and at annual meetings delegates discussed issues that threatened workers: among them, immigrants taking on jobs at low wages, thereby lowering Canadian workers' income potential and taking jobs away from them. Only six years after Confederation, Canada had an entrenched identity, and many newcomers, even if they were from the mother country, were regarded as unwelcome intruders. In fact, it's interesting that by the early 1880s, and earlier in some cases, in Canada's press and government reports, the word *emigrant* was gradually being replaced by *immigrant*. Emigrants are people who leave their own country for a new one; immigrants are people who have settled *in* a country from somewhere else. After just a few years, Canadians had enough self-confidence to relate newcomers to their own country, not to Great Britain.

In September 1883, the Trades and Labour Council, headed up by Charles March, issued a report that attacked the Canadian government's continued efforts to draw immigrants to Canada, arguing that the policy was detrimental to both Canadians and the immigrants themselves. According to the report, compiled by the council's legislative committee, there had been a recent meeting in Birmingham, England, organized by that country's Trades and Labour Congress, and it was suggested at that gathering that there was plenty of "waste land" in Britain that could be cultivated by those who were considering emigrating to the colonies. By encouraging migration (movement within England), the wave of emigration could be halted. Using this information, the Canadian report went on to list various trades — bricklayers, stonemasons, carpenters, and joiners among them — and assessed the employment climate for each one. It determined that in most cases, supply exceeded demand,

and so there was no need to import labour to Canada. Of particular concern to the council was that destitute and undesirable emigrants were being sent to Canada, and it stressed that these were not the sort of newcomers who should be allowed into the country.[16]

Anti-immigration sentiment had decidedly racist undertones, as well. There was an unpleasant backlash against poor Irish emigrants pouring into Toronto and other centres, but an even greater one toward Chinese labour that had been imported to build the CPR. By 1885, these Chinese workers were now drifting eastward, as the railway had been completed that year. In a July 20, 1885, report in the *Globe* by a correspondent writing from British Columbia, it was noted that the Chinese now took on such tasks as laundering, waiting on tables, and mending — jobs that unmarried or widowed Canadian women traditionally did. The author warned that very soon the Chinese would be travelling east to centres such as Toronto and Hamilton, and their businesses would supplant those of Canadians. Despite the unpleasant aspect of this reaction to Irish and Chinese immigrants, trade unionists' criticism of all immigration efforts indicated that there was more at stake, at least in their eyes, than a simple dislike of "foreigners."

That same year, the federal government offered $350,000 toward assisted passages, and protests were renewed. An 1885 report from the Legislative Committee of the Trades and Labour Council was especially critical. "There is no justifiable reason for the expenditure during the coming year, of such an enormous sum of the public money as $350,000 in the assisting of poor people to this country, or the employing of an army of travelling and other immigration agents in Great Britain and on the continent of Europe."[17] The council may have had a point. At the time, British-based emigration societies were flourishing, and steamship lines — particularly the Allan, based in Montreal — had been actively recruiting emigrants with cheap passages since the early 1850s. The report also suggested the economic depression in Canada made it an inappropriate destination for emigrants looking for work. It could be that the report's contention that the provincial and federal emigration agents were simply exploiting their employers as they languished in the great cities of Britain and mainland Europe was justified. However, the tide of immigration could not be stopped, and Ontario's, and Canada's, population continued to be increased by immigration despite the protests from the labour community.

By the 1880s, Ontario was, of course, no longer regarding itself as chiefly an agricultural province, as early proponents of the free grant scheme had designated it. Industry and commerce, especially in the major centres such as Toronto, London, and Hamilton, required a healthy population, and immigrants brought their trades and expertise to these cities. No longer were poor British emigrants from inner-city neighbourhoods being sent to labour on a free grant lot in Muskoka — they had the option of working in urban centres. The quaint warnings of the early days of emigration to Ontario — that cities were hotbeds of vice and temptations — no longer held water. As these new immigrants settled in Toronto and other cities in the province, they, too, would begin to regard Muskoka solely as a holiday destination.

Chapter Nine

The Waning Days of the Free Grant Scheme

*Clearings which had once borne more or less of a crop were grown up
again, and their wildness was as the wildness of the forest primeval.*[1]
— Frederick de la Fosse, *English Bloods*

John A. Macdonald's dream of a national railway in Canada had a powerful effect on the future of Muskoka's free grant scheme, for as the Canadian Pacific Railway snaked across the country, it became increasingly important for the Northern Railway to link up with the main CPR line. Free grant lands had already opened up in northwestern Ontario, as well as in Manitoba, and at the same time, the fertile clay belt in the northern district of Nipissing was being touted as the next prime agricultural destination. Muskoka's easy accessibility continued to draw tourists, but now other regions, deemed more attractive as farming destinations, were just as accessible. This flurry of railway building meant that wherever the railway decided to construct stations along the line, a whistle-stop town soon mushroomed in its vicinity. And while these towns began to flourish, the small hamlets in Muskoka began to decline. A case in point was Hoodstown, just west of Lake Vernon. Founded with expectations of the railway passing through the town, Hoodstown was rejected in favour of Huntsville, then a busy centre, and it virtually disappeared from the map.

Celebrating the completion of the Northern Railway's final journey from the town of Callender to connect to the CPR at North Bay, the *Globe* featured a two-part article in late December 1886 and January 1887, titled "The Callender Extension." Linking the Northern Railway to the CPR would make a huge impact on Canada's development, connecting the major city of Toronto with the country's west coast. The first article followed the train as it chugged between Toronto and Orillia; the second, on January 29, focused on the region north of Orillia, through the free grant lands and on to North Bay. Muskoka, the article suggested, was a place to "enjoy perfect freedom from the restraints of fashionable life." Descriptions of the businesses, hotels, schools, and churches in each Muskoka community suggested that they were, indeed, thriving: Gravenhurst's stores and houses were described as "handsome and tasteful in appearance"; Bracebridge was so prosperous that "[t]here are few points in Ontario that offer such splendid facilities for manufacturing purposes, as the water power is practically unlimited and always certain;" and in Huntsville, "The larger part of the land in the neighborhood has been taken up under the Free Grants Act, and the settlers are rapidly becoming wealthy." The author didn't identify just who these "wealthy" settlers were — it seems his descriptive powers were on the wane by the time he reached Hunstville.

The author then went on to repeat that old chestnut: although the land was rocky and barren along the roads, *beyond* those roads, the land was sixty percent arable. This was a handy explanation that had been used by many, but W.E. Hamilton, in his *Muskoka Sketch* pamphlet of 1880, commented on the irony of the claim. Despite his endorsement of rock as a growing medium in his Muskoka atlas, he was rather amused by the phrase "at the back," as in, the good land is "at the back." Presumably the term was used as a reassurance whenever a settler first set eyes on the rocky frontage of his lot and expressed some dismay. Hamilton noted, "Even where this good back land was invisible, you were always told to believe in its existence, just as the unseen side of the moon may be shaped and level."[2] Actually, the *Globe's* article scarcely mentioned agricultural issues or the free grant lands in particular — the commercial aspect of the region was its main focus. The small nod toward Huntsville's free grant lands was merely mentioned in passing, and consequently the author felt free to exaggerate the success of the scheme. Sadly, the truth didn't really matter anymore, as it once had. There was no longer a need to convince settlers to farm Muskoka, and the myth that so many farmers were prosperous would be challenged by few.

How disheartening it must have been for poorer farmers who might have read the article. Everyone — the government, the free grant advocates, and the press — seemed to have turned a blind eye to their plight.

~

One way of assessing the dwindling fortunes of the free grant lands is by considering a Department of Agriculture report in 1887, which gave a breakdown of immigrants' destinations in the past year. Whereas 2,364 went to Manitoba, only seventy-two ended up in Muskoka. Other immigrants, in numbers ranging from 7 to 247, went on to Hastings, Simcoe, Bruce, and Waterloo. Of those seventy-two immigrants who settled in Muskoka, one could conjecture that a good number were relatives or friends of settlers already there, as the free grant lands were no longer the major focus of the government or of emigration agents. Immigrants who had been involved in their home country's hospitality industry might have seen potential in the tourist trade and its offshoots in Muskoka. What the statistics do show us is that the district was failing to bring in much in the way of new blood.

Not only were the numbers of settlers diminishing, the value of farms whose land had proved to be unsuitable for agriculture would have been negligible, thus restricting a farmer's ability to relocate. By the turn of the century, settlers who had arrived in Muskoka from the early days of the free grant scheme would be well into middle age or older. With their farms representing very little capital, their desire to sell up would be dashed, and many were probably forced to stay on land that had reaped very little profit over the course of their lives.

Over the ensuing decades, Ontario's free grant scheme remained in place, although it was altered over the course of the years. In 1941, free grants were suspended for ordinary settlers, and were reserved for military veterans, who were bestowed grants as a reward for service — much as they were in the early days of Upper Canada. These free grants were mainly located in the Kenora and Rainy River districts, and allowances for swamps and rocky land were made in the form of extra acreage. Sounds familiar, doesn't it? Incredibly, the mistake of settling farmers on poor land was being repeated even at this late date. Needless to say, Muskoka was no longer on the list of districts still open for settlement — lots with water frontage would be too valuable to give away by then, and as farmers had learned, inland lots were generally unfit for agriculture.

~

In the lottery of free grant life, there were, of course, those who prospered. Settlers with adequate farming skills and with fertile land were bound to succeed in Muskoka. Many of the others, ones whose land was infertile, could relocate if they had capital or simple wherewithal. Four of the memoirists I have cited in earlier chapters did just that. Mrs. Copleston, the woman who admitted she had arrived in the bush near Orillia without even knowing how to bake a loaf of bread, was thankful to eventually relocate to a fertile farm on the St. Lawrence River. Harriet Barbara King, who was capable in the kitchen but unable to deal with the hardship of free grant farming, was also luckier than many. In 1874, her youngest son became a schoolmaster in Allensville, a nearby village. Her daughter and son-in-law, J.S. Cole, moved to Bracebridge, where he was the incumbent at St. Thomas' Anglican Church from 1874 to 1883. Her son Charles, who had first enticed Mrs. King to Muskoka, was appointed postmaster in Lancelot in 1877, a position he held until 1881. King might have enjoyed a little melodrama, but she had nothing to gain by exaggerating her troubled life in the bush. She could have written a glowing account, and her book, like Catharine Parr Traill's, might have received the endorsement of the Canadian emigration agents. Near the end of *Letters from Muskoka*, she wrote: "I went into the bush of Muskoka strong and healthy, full of life and energy, and fully as enthusiastic as the youngest of our party. I left it with hopes completely crushed, and with health so hopelessly shattered from hard work, unceasing anxiety and trouble of all kinds, that I am now a helpless invalid, entirely confined by the doctor's orders to my bed and sofa, without the remotest chance of ever leaving them for a more active life during the remainder of my days on earth."[3] Bitterly, she claimed, "We had long looked upon Bush life in the light of exile to a penal settlement without even the convict's chance of a ticket-to-leave."[4] As it turned out, her "ticket" did arrive, for eventually she and members of her family ended up in Toronto. She died in 1885 and was buried in Toronto's Mount Pleasant Cemetery.

Thomas Osborne, who had arrived in Muskoka in 1875, left the bush for good in 1879, leaving behind his father, William, and brother Arthur, and returning to his mother and siblings in Philadelphia. His father refused to join them and remained on the land until his death in 1913 at the age of ninety-two. Osborne's father and brother Arthur were quite resourceful. They ran a stage wagon service between North and South Portage for some years, linking Mary Lake with Lake of Bays. Thomas Osborne also lived a long life: he died in Philadelphia at the age of eighty-nine after being struck by a car. In his memoir, he claimed that he had arrived in Muskoka at age fifteen, weighing sixty-five pounds; when he returned to Philadelphia five years later, he weighed 185. Clearly bush life had made a man of him — despite his hardships.

Frederick de la Fosse, who was sent from England to Muskoka to learn bush farming, claimed his own free grant and farmed for the next nine or so years. He eventually became Peterborough, Ontario's first public librarian in 1910, and died in 1950 at the age of ninety.[5] The opening quote of this chapter arose from a visit he made to Muskoka, probably in the late 1920s. Where once he had enjoyed the companionship of the many settlers he had shared bush life with, there was now a melancholy emptiness. He mused, "That the experience spoilt the careers of most of us goes without saying. We spent nine or ten years of the most valuable period of our lives in wrestling with the timber and undergoing many of the drawbacks inseparable from a settler's existence in a new country."[6] Despite attempting to write a lighthearted account of backwoods life in Muskoka, de la Fosse concluded, "Many events I have purposely omitted to chronicle in these recollections. They were of too poignant a character, and no purpose would be served by mentioning them.... Some of our nearest and dearest friends passed away under the saddest of conditions. One by one, the remainder left the district."[7]

Despite the difficulties they had endured, Copleston, King, Osborne, and de la Fosse escaped the bush and were able in varying degrees to rebuild their lives after many difficulties. The very existence of their memoirs shows that educated settlers who had led relatively privileged lives in their homelands saw no reason to continue a life of hardship. Those they left behind, the ones who had been dealt a bad hand when land was apportioned and who were unable to escape, were less fortunate. At least these memoirists saw fit to describe the hardships and tragedies many had experienced in the bush, for those left behind had been abandoned by almost everyone else.

~

A recurring theme in this book is that no one took responsibility for the misfortunes of free grant settlers, with the exception of the agricultural commissioners who visited Muskoka in 1880 and hinted that the architects of the free grant scheme were responsible for the bad policy. The people responsible for the free grant policy — the emigration enthusiasts, politicians, and businessmen — who had handily engineered the settlers' destinies, simply got on with their lives. John Sandfield Macdonald died just a few years after the free grant scheme, and admittedly before the real deficiencies of the scheme had been widely reported upon. Stephen Richards's political career was fairly short-lived. He left politics in 1874 and practiced law for some time in Toronto. Suffering from ill health, he spent most of his later years in France. He returned to Toronto a few years before his sudden death at the Toronto Island ferry terminal. John Sandfield Macdonald's successor, Edward Blake, went on to federal politics, where, over time, he was minister of justice and president of the Privy Council. He later sat in the British House of Commons as an Irish Nationalist MP, but finally returned to Canada to be a senator and chancellor at the University of Toronto. Oliver Mowat was knighted in 1892 and became lieutenant governor of Ontario in 1897. He supported free grant schemes throughout the province during his entire career, despite the fact that many were in the far northwestern reaches of the province, which, similar to Muskoka, were not the most fertile of regions. John Carling became a federal minister of agriculture from 1885 to 1892, was president of the family's brewing business, and was eventually knighted. A.P. Cockburn's political life was stormy, but his fleet of steamships flourished and he continued his energetic support of Muskoka as a tourist destination.

Perhaps it is naïve to believe that a little mea culpa was in order. But the game of politics is to continually move on; had Oliver Mowat stood up in the Legislature and admitted his party had erred in judgement in touting Muskoka as an agricultural district, he may never have enjoyed his long tenure in office. Self-interest got in the way of compassion and common sense, and the free grant architects were not the ones who paid the price for gross miscalculations regarding Muskoka's suitability for agricultural settlement.

Thomas McMurray left Muskoka for Toronto in 1879, where he continued his temperance activities. Little is known about his life after that, except that in 1884, he turned up in the Eastern Townships of Quebec, where he was associated with the Grand Division of Quebec of the Sons of Temperance. The Parry Sound *North Star*, his old newspaper, announced his death in its August 23, 1900, edition. Although probably well-intentioned, McMurray had made wild estimations of the fertility of Muskoka's soil and had scorned his critics. For all that he had accomplished in Muskoka, through his businesses, newspapers, and guidebook, he never experienced the suffering that many of the settlers endured. A highly inventive man, he was free to re-establish himself even after numerous setbacks.

W.E. Hamilton eventually settled in Chatham, Ontario, in the southwestern region of the province, where he continued his career in journalism. His endorsement of the free grant district in his *Guide Book & Atlas* was likely driven more by financial needs than altruism, for he had little enthusiasm for settling in the bush himself. In his memoir, *Peeps at My Life*, he summed up his Muskoka experience succinctly. "After residence in Toronto and Meaford, I migrated to Parry Sound, took up a free grant, got sick of it and settled in Bracebridge."[8] Despite his unhappy free grant experience, he immortalized Muskoka in his *Muskoka Sketch* and his atlas. In an article published in the *Irish Astronomical Journal* in 1999, author P.A. Wayman critiqued the life of Hamilton, placing him in the context of having had a brilliant father — Sir William Rowan Hamilton, a mathematical genius of his time — but never reaching the heights of scholarly ambition himself. Hamilton died in 1902, either on the streets of Chatham (Wayman's account) or in one of the city's public houses (Hamilton's obituary in the *Globe*). Old age had caught on with him, apparently, as Wayman described him as "a shuffling old man in a ragged overcoat."[9] Hamilton's literary skills and ironic sense of humour were exemplified in his memoir's last sentence: "And now, gentle reader goodbye. Come on Mr. Critic and cut me up like a pig, as Tennyson used to say: Sharpen your knife. My hide is thickened by thirty years of journalism."[10]

Styleman Herring, as we have seen, was the one person who seemed to have shown some self-discipline early on — by 1874, he decided to stop the flow of his emigrants to the free grant lands, although he went on to blithely send others off to Manitoba with an equal lack of knowledge of the province. His address at the Royal Colonial Institute in 1881 revealed that he was reluctant to comment on free land offered by the colonies, which suggests the free grant scheme was a subject he wished to forget. He remained engaged in emigration endeavours throughout his lifetime, and carried on with his parish duties and philanthropic works until his death in 1896. Herring's dogged enthusiasm for the free grant scheme and his seeming silence when irrefutable evidence emerged that the scheme should never have been contemplated remains puzzling. He was a pivotal character in the early days and perhaps the most influential in advocating the free grant scheme to emigration advocates in England. So why, until 1874, did he continue with a scheme that early on came under attack? He may have been simply gullible, believing his hosts when they told him that the settlers were all doing well and not questioning why there were contrary reports that contradicted their assertions. And he must have believed his Muskoka hosts' assurances that the district was up to 70 percent fertile, but that the fertile land was out of sight of the roads and lakes he had travelled upon. Or perhaps he saw the poverty that existed but refused to believe it was due to Muskoka's unfit land and still attributed settlers' lack of success to their own misdeeds — whether intemperance, laziness, or a refusal to adapt to Canadian farming practices. Herring was an intelligent man, but perhaps a proud one. Most likely, he was silent because he simply couldn't bring himself to accept that he had been a party, however innocent, to the free grant scheme. There were enough successful settlers across other districts in Ontario for him to put on a brave face and accept his hero's welcome in Canada.

The dire poverty Herring encountered every day cannot be exaggerated, and the impact of such want would have motivated his belief that the free grant lands, whether or not entirely fertile, would provide a better life than the hellish streets in his parish. The depression in Britain of the late 1860s brought a good deal of misery to his parish in Clerkenwell, and even thirty years later, parts of his parish were still steeped in poverty. Charles Booth, a British businessman and social reformer, spent several years with a team of investigators to detail levels of wealth and poverty in London. The resulting seventeen-volume publication, *Life and Labour of the People in London (1886–1903)*, contained maps of each street, which were colour-coded to indicate categories of income. Although much of the neighbourhood surrounding St Paul's, Clerkenwell, showed some prosperity, two streets in particular, Peartree and Bastwick, which run directly east of Herring's parish church, were designated as extremely poor with frequent crime. In the thirty years since Herring had first founded his emigration society, little had changed for the lives of his parishioners. Faced with such grinding poverty day after day, year after year, Herring would have been desperate to change the course of those people's lives.

Just months before Herring's death, an editorial in *Reynolds's Newspaper* admonished him for war-mongering. It isn't stated which war, but this was the time of the Jameson Raids in the Transvaal, which led up to the Second Boer War. According to *Reynolds's*, Herring had sent the editor a message that read, "One cheer more for old England. We have got the money, and we have got the ships, and we won't stand any more nonsense from anywhere, or anybody."[11] On January 12, the paper replied, "This peaceful appeal is very rousing and comes oddly from a follower of 'Gentle Jesus, meek and mild.' Jingo parsons were more wanted in the bad old times of the Crusades than now-a-days." Herring's remarks did seem rather bellicose for a vicar. Perhaps Herring was ill, however, and he had grown crankier in old age, for he died the following June. Short obituaries in the British press praised his good works, his frequent open-air preaching, and, especially, his role in sending more than five thousand emigrants to the colonies.

Epilogue

The High Cost of Free Land

[Muskoka] is designed to be an important manufacturing country,
and may one day be the very workshop of Canada itself.[1]
— Thomas McMurray, *The Free Grant Lands of Canada*

Speculations that Muskoka would eventually become a major agri-cultural centre proved to be hugely optimistic, but there *is* a healthy farming community in Muskoka today, if much smaller than anticipated by the early free grant proponents. Luckily, the current interest in buying local produce has been a boon for these farmers. Two websites, Muskoka Farm Fresh and Savour Muskoka, celebrate the thriving culinary trad-itions of the district, revealing that even limited amounts of fertile land can support a farming community. And yet, a drive through Muskoka's quiet back roads, away from the resorts and cottages, hardly reveals a pastoral landscape. The farms are scattered on the rare fertile belts that can sustain them, sometimes with miles of dense bush in between. When one compares these farms with the ones listed in W.E. Hamilton's 1879 atlas, which were hemmed in by their neighbours, it is poignantly obvious that the district failed to fulfill the early settlers' dreams. And as the bush has long grown over what were once small clearings, it is diffi-cult to reconcile today's landscape with the expectations of Hamilton and other free grant supporters.

During the course of my research, I met several people who were free grant descendants, and the lasting emotional impact of the scheme was a frequent topic in our discussions. One person stands out in particular. A ninety-year-old friend of my mother's told me the tale of her late husband's family, who had left their home in England to settle a free grant near Huntsville. Although almost one hundred and fifty years had passed since then, she still expressed anger at those who had lured the family to Muskoka. The farm was infertile, and facing starvation and with no steady income, they resorted to peeling bark off their trees to sell to a local tannery. This had been a terrible come-down for a family who had had visions of a better life in Canada. When I located the lot on Hamilton's atlas, I wondered how many of their neighbours had found themselves in similar circumstances. An entire community had virtually disappeared.

The Free Grants Act has had repercussions, admittedly somewhat indirectly, well into the twenty-first century. Although from its very beginning, tourism alleviated the financial woes of many of Muskoka's citizens, the prosperity was not, and has not, been shared by all. The October/November 2004 issue of *Muskoka Magazine*, an attractive glossy periodical that highlights lifestyle and community aspects of the district, featured an article by the late Carolyn Bray, who had been the executive director of the district's YWCA before her untimely death in 2009. Amid pieces on local museum displays, wild turkeys, local artists, and local food, her article, "The Domino Effect," stood alone. In it, she aptly demonstrated how a region dependent on a tourist economy would be at risk. Bray was addressing a previous provincial government's re-designation of Muskoka as a "southern" community, no longer to enjoy the social and development programs offered by the ministry of Northern Development and Mines. Decrying the image of Muskoka merely as a destination for the wealthy, Bray contended in her article that the district was in many ways a disadvantaged one.

She described Muskoka's lack of affordable housing, and explained that many of its citizens could find only seasonal employment, or were either under-employed, self-employed, or simply unemployed. And because of the influx of tourists and cottagers, property values had skyrocketed, meaning for some, more than fifty percent of household income could be spent on housing itself. Public transit was also inadequate in the district, which resulted in decreased mobility for those without vehicles of their own. These difficulties, she claimed, inevitably led to domestic abuse and petty crime. Bray compared Muskoka to Whistler, B.C., where there have been similar problems with low-income employees working in a high-income, largely seasonal resort. Whistler's high cost of living meant that low-income employees often found themselves unable to make ends meet, and consequently, ran afoul of the law. To address this concern, the police and federal, provincial, and municipal authorities, as well as Intrawest, Whistler's main employer at that time, had made a concerted effort to establish social programs to counteract this problem. Such a solution would be difficult for Muskoka, as it is not a "company" town, but there are signs that some of Bray's concerns have been addressed. Working with the Ontario Municipal Social Services Association, the Poverty Reduction of Muskoka Planning Team (PROMPT) today addresses issues such as domestic violence, lack of affordable housing, and the growing need for food banks.

Author Brett Grainger wrote a more personal account of the district with "The Other Muskoka," an article published in the July 2005 issue of *Toronto Life*. Grainger is a descendant of Thomas Gray, who arrived in Muskoka from England in 1872 to claim his free grant, and his heritage enabled him to speak freely about the disturbing legacy of the free grant scheme. He described decades-long feuds among some of the district's families, many still living on the free grant lots of their ancestors. As he saw it, years of poverty, which began during the free grant years, had robbed his own generation of opportunities available to those in more affluent parts of the province. When Grainger visited the site of his ancestors' free grant lot, he was deeply moved by the futility of their lives and the broken promises that they had fallen victim to. At least one Muskoka resident wrote a letter to the editor of the magazine, concerned that Grainger had been ridiculing Muskoka residents, but that person had missed the point of Grainger's article: he wasn't ridiculing the local population; he was attributing their difficulties in part to the free grant scheme, and the decades of poverty that later ensued. Incidentally, Grainger won a National Magazine Award for this moving take on a different aspect of today's Muskoka.

~

The free grant scheme certainly disproved the complaint by some that Ontario history is dull: there was nothing dull about the province during those early years of settlement. One can't help but be struck by the colourful characters who wandered the Muskoka bush in the 1870s. Thomas McMurray was unafraid to try his hand at anything — including pioneering, politics, and commerce — to raise both Muskoka's stature and his own, a trait which must have impressed all but the poorer settlers on their disappointing free grant of land. The dashing Colonel Francis Cornwallis Maude, with his lavish entertaining and hunting parties, was another anomaly in the backwoods. With his tales of the Indian Mutiny and possession of a Victoria Cross, he must have cut quite a figure. Even more eccentric was W.E. Hamilton, the scholar and newspaperman, with his pet snowy owl and birch-bark accessories, holed up with his books and, perhaps, his bottles above the *Free Grant Gazette.* The cranky Horrocks Cocks, whose emigration initiatives were spurned by both John Carling and Archibald McKellar, spent some time in Muskoka; his rather outlandish name alone must have drawn some attention.

Styleman Herring was one of the most unexpected participants in the free grant scheme. Who would have thought a vicar from an East End London slum would become integral to the free grant scheme? His boyish enthusiasm, his willingness to trust his Canadian advisers, his life-long quest to better the lives of the poor and afflicted, and most important, his prescient withdrawal from the free grant scheme make him one of the most admirable characters in this book. For just as the Ontario legislators had high hopes and mostly honourable intentions in the early days of the scheme, Herring was quick to envision a new community where the poor could find a decent home.

This story also afforded us a glimpse at the ceremonies and celebrations of life in nineteenth century cities and towns in Ontario. Pomp and ceremony ran rampant on February 28, 1868, the day the Free Grants Act was passed, when Ontario's lieutenant governor arrived at the Legislature in Toronto, with one hundred members of the Thirteenth Hussars and an equal number of the Seventeenth Regiment greeting him with their military bands. The province of Ontario was just about eight months old — the excitement and reverence for the Legislature's important business was duly recognized. Who can forget the crisp September evening in 1870 when those Muskoka movers-and-shakers and their guests stepped off the Bracebridge dock to blazing bonfires, hearty cheers, and a special banquet at the Dominion House? It was an evening of rousing speeches, applause, and bonhomie, with the revelry lasting into the early-morning hours. In August 1874, Lord and Lady Dufferin were greeted in Gravenhurst with banners and flags and a pine-bough archway as the townspeople gathered to meet their special guests. Another grand occasion in Gravenhurst was the arrival of the railway in November 1875, when the train brought the president and directors of the Northern Railway Company to the town to celebrate this grand event. Imagine that ear-splitting, five-minute-long steam-whistle salute in concert with the brass band that simultaneously welcomed the dignitaries. These events, whether in Toronto or the Muskoka backwoods, were the very essence of nineteenth-century Ontario society.

Sadly, many of the settlers who lived in remote areas of the free grant lands probably had little to do with the colourful characters and joyous celebrations throughout the 1870s and later. For those isolated men and women, life would have remained unchanged, with often little to celebrate. And so while some were enjoying the fruits of Muskoka settlement, there were many others who lived out their lives in quiet desperation.

∽

Even had the warnings about the unsuitability of Muskoka for agricultural settlement been considered more carefully, it is doubtful that the scheme would have been abandoned. In the early days of the free grant scheme, agriculture was the only viable means of support new settlers lacking an education or trade would have had. Other than lumbering, which was not an ideal occupation for the head of a household — it was seasonal work that demanded prolonged absences from the family — there was little commercial infrastructure in the vast Ottawa-Huron tract, and little demand for business ventures until the towns and villages grew. As we have seen, agricultural settlement was the enticement given to lure emigrants to Australia with early lack of success, and the same means was employed by the United States to people the western prairies. Little consideration was given as to whether or not the land being settled was fertile, or if these settlers would prosper, for there was a larger agenda at stake — populating empty territories.

Once the free grant scheme was initiated, there was no going back. Admission that the scheme was ill advised would have been political suicide for the politicians who supported it, and financially disastrous for business-men, most notably A.P. Cockburn and Thomas McMurray, who had much to lose if they admitted defeat. In the absence of a welfare state, there was little one could do to help those who were not thriving. The best alternative was to continue to build the commercial infrastructure of the small urban centres and blame those who were struggling for their own misfortunes. Once tourism became a reality in Muskoka, an entirely new perspective on the district's commercial viability became evident, and the free grant settlers faded into the background.

In Britain, the work of emigration philanthropists was guaranteed to continue until governments ceased their laissez-faire attitudes toward fixing social problems such as poverty: the refusal of state authorities to consider the many delegations made by emigration adherents throughout the 1870s demonstrated their willingness to leave such a pressing matter to amateurs. That is surprising, for at the same time, there was no great enthusiasm for populating workhouses and paying poor rates, but surprising or not, that was the path chosen by successive British governments. What seemed to be in play was a reluctance to get further involved in Canada's affairs — it was fine and well if emigration agents and philanthropists wished to send the poor to Canada, but Britain, with its rapid industrialization, was more focused on its own prosperous future and empirical aspirations than with the overseas settlement of the country's poor.

If this story of Muskoka settlement had been written as a traditional hist-ory, it would have focused solely on the powerful men who devised the free grant scheme, the politicians and businessmen who helped the towns and villages flourish, and the emigration proponents who sent people to the vast empty stretches of the Ottawa-Huron tract. But the story would have been incomplete without additional focus on the emigrant settlers whose very destinies were decided by those above them on the social ladder.

A few decades ago, history was taught largely from the top down. The emphasis was on the men — and it *was* usually men — who were political and business leaders. One of my professors in the 1970s referred to social history as "what the peasants ate for breakfast." Thankfully, exclusively top-down history has been largely replaced by a "bottom-up" approach, a study that focuses on issues of race, gender, and/or class, and linking those issues within a historical framework. In the case of Muskoka's free grant history, it is precisely the fact that the "peasant" class often *wasn't* eating much for breakfast that is central to a full knowledge of the subject. While the actions of the men central to this story must be addressed, as the legislators, emigration agents, and businessmen were vital players in the history of the free grants, it is important to learn what the consequences of their decisions were. The history of Muskoka couldn't be adequately told without addressing emigration settlement as well.

While beginning my research on the graduate thesis that became the inspiration for this book, I found that there was a scarcity of historical literature on the subject of nineteenth-century emigrants and emigration societies in Great Britain, with some exceptions. Most books expounded on policy and policy-makers, not on the emigrants themselves. Howard L. Malchow's *Population Pressures: Emigration and Government in Late Nineteenth-Century Britain*, published in 1979, was a useful source, but it failed to follow the emigrants to their new land — his mention of Styleman Herring was gratifying but unfulfilling, as there was no information on how his emigration society's members fared once they reached Canada or New Zealand. The lack of information on the emigrants themselves in the historical canon could be that emigrants weren't deemed worthy of much attention by historians or the countries they hearkened from. Eric Richards addressed this point well in his *Britannia's Children: Emigration from England, Scotland, Wales and Ireland Since 1600*, a comprehensive look at child emigration. He suggested that most emigrants were "invisible," that they lacked political clout, were often illiterate, and usually poor. In fact, he noted that they were often regarded as the "white trash" of British society. Strong words, but they shed light on why Styleman Herring had such difficulty in persuading either the British or Ontario governments to give financial aid for emigration programs — no one seemed especially bothered about the fate of society's poor.

The Muskoka that visitors see today is a very different one from the days of the free grants. There is little evidence that thousands of settlers once attempted to farm their acres of soil in a region now filled with cottages and resorts. In fact, Muskoka has been virtually expropriated from its local inhabitants, many of whom are free grant descendants. In the rest of the province, the press has reverted to calling the district, and others similar to it, "cottage country," as if Muskoka exists merely as a playground for southerners, thereby losing its autonomy as a region with a distinct history. The free grant settlers who settled the district paid a high cost for their free land. With this book, I have attempted to give them the voice and recognition they rarely have been afforded.

Acknowledgements

A heartfelt thank you to all the staff at Dundurn for their acceptance of a first-time author and for helping make *Hardscrabble* a reality. It has also been a great pleasure working with my editor, Laura Harris.

Special thanks to J. Patrick Boyer for his unstinting encouragement and support for *Hardscrabble*. Mary Stokes, Elizabeth MacLean, Neil Hester, Michael Doucet, Margaret Learn, and Susan Girvan have offered insights and suggestions for *Hardscrabble*. Katherine LaRocca was my diligent fact-checker. Nancy Holtz, a reference librarian at the Bracebridge Public Library, kindly guided me through the Muskoka Collection archives. Professors Lori Loeb, my M.A. adviser, and Laurel MacDowell, who supervised my initial independent studies thesis, were instrumental in the early development of this book. Ian Denning from London, England, sent me a copy of Styleman Herring's calling card, and graciously gave permission for its reproduction. Ted Currie and Scott Shipman are Muskoka historians who have kindly shared their knowledge of the district. Thanks also to Father Barry Oake, vicar of the parish church of Thorpe St. Andrew, Norwich, who kindly gave my husband and me a tour of the church.

Finally, I would like to thank many members of my family. Lawrence Williams, my cousin and a retired lecturer at the University of Dundee, kindly edited the first draft of the manuscript. My brother Bruce Williams researched British aspects of my story from his home in Balloch, Scotland, and created the map of Muskoka. My husband, John Ward, and my eldest brother, John Williams, read excerpts of *Hardscrabble* and encouraged me throughout this lengthy project. Thanks to my sister-in-law Deb O'Rourke, who commiserated with me as she wrote her own first book. My mother, Elizabeth, who died just months before the publication of *Hardscrabble* at the age of ninety-four, was a stalwart throughout, eagerly anticipating the book. And finally, Emma and Joe, who have probably suffered most throughout the past years with a distracted mother who had the nerve to apply to the University of Toronto at the same time they did!

Thank you, all.

Notes

Chapter One

1   Charles Marshall, *The Canadian Dominion*, 55.

2   *Ibid.*

3   Thomas McMurray, *The Free Grant Lands of Canada*, 83.

4   T.P. French, *Information for Intending Settlers on the Ottawa and Opeongo Road, And Its Vicinity*, 6.

5   Florence Murray, *Muskoka and Haliburton 1615–1875: A Collection of Documents*, "R.J. Oliver, 'Report on the Muskoka Road, 1862,'" 252.

6   The Parry Sound district was included in the region under debate, but generally the politicians just referred to "Muskoka."

7   In the days before the Legislature debates were recorded in Hansard, they were copied by newspaper reporters and published the following day. I have followed the debates as they were reported in the Toronto *Globe*. The paper's reporter paraphrased the speeches, and so quoted material in the text is directly quoted from the *Globe*, not from the member of the Legislature in question. I have greatly condensed the material in these debates, while striving to convey the tenor and earnestness of the speeches.

8 Murray, *Muskoka and Haliburton*, "Alexander Shirreff's Exploration from the Ottawa River to Georgian Bay, 1829," 71.

9 Murray, *Muskoka and Haliburton*, "Bell to Commissioner of Crown Lands, J.H. Price, 1848," 147.

10 *Ibid.*, 148.

11 *Ibid.*, "J. Stoughton Dennis's 'Report … of the Survey of The Muskoka Road Line, North of Grand Falls, Parry Sound Road Line, & Exploration to Mouth of Muskoka River,'" 169.

12 *Ibid.*, "Vernon B. Wadsworth's 'Reminiscences of Surveys, 1860–64,'" 177.

13 Douglas W. Hoffman and Henry F. Noble, *Acreages of Soil Capability Classes for Agriculture in Ontario*, 1, 2, 134.

14 Murray, *Muskoka and Haliburton*, "J.W. Bridgland's 'Report … of Exploring Lines from the Eldon Portage to the Mouth of the River Muskoka,' January 31, 1853," 151–5.

15 Charles Landy MacDermott, *Facts for Emigrants: A Journey from London to the Backwoods of Canada*, 12.

Chapter Two

1 Harriet Barbara King, *Letters from Muskoka by an Emigrant Lady*, 272.

2 Information on agents is sourced from Patrick A. Dunae's article from *Archivaria 19*, "Promoting the Dominion: Records and the Canadian Immigration Campaign, 1872-1915," 73–93. *http://journals.sfu.ca/archivar/index.php/archivaria/article/view/11135/12072*. Also, "Enticing the Emigrant: Canadian Agents in Ireland and Scotland, c. 1870–c. 1920," by Marjory Harper, in the *Scottish Historical Review*, vol. LXXXIII, 1: No. 215: April 2004, 41–58. *http://www.euppublishing.com/doi/abs/10.3366/shr.2004.83.1.41*.

3 *Emigration to Canada: The The Province of Ontario* (1869), 22.

4 McMurray, *The Free Grant Lands of Canada*, 95.

5   *Ibid.*, 96.

6   Sadly, the church was badly damaged in 1940 during the Blitz and the congregation merged with nearby St. Luke's in 1953, after which it was torn down.

7   Styleman Herring, *Nearly Forty Years Exclusively Among the Poor of London*, 59.

8   Lady Hobart, *Help for the Helpless: London's Bitter Cry Hushed in Canada*, Early Canadiana Online, *http://www.canadiana.org/ECO/ mtq?doc=16796*, 7.

9   Ontario, *Sessional Papers*, 33 Victoria 1869 (no. 12), 4.

10 Herring, *Emigration for Poor Folks*, 1.

11 *Ibid.*, 9.

12 Ontario *Sessional Papers*, 33 Victoria 1869 (no. 45), 10.

13 Samuel Smiles, *Self-Help*, 295.

14 Joseph Nelson, *Emigration to North America: A Letter to the Right Honourable G. J. Goschen, M.P., President of the Poor Law Board*, 11.

15 *Biograph and Review*, "Rev. A. Styleman Herring, M.A.," 609.

16 Edward Jenkins, *State Emigration: An Essay*, 16.

17 *Ibid.*, 50.

Chapter Three

1   Herring, *Emigration to the British Colonies*. This song doesn't appear in my photocopy of the book; it was an adjunct to the pamphlet as copied on microfilm at the Archives of Ontario.

2   Thomas White, *A Lecture on Canada as a Field for Emigration*, 15.

3   Alexander Kirkwood and J.J. Murphy, *The Undeveloped Lands in Northern & Western Ontario*, 39.

4   McMurray, *The Free Grant Lands of Canada*, 42.

5   From Immigrants to Canada website: *http://retirees.uwaterloo.ca/ ~marj/genealogy/prussianfare.html.*

6   Hobart, *Help for the Helpless*, 8.

7   Herring, *Letters from Abroad and Hints to Emigrants*, 5–7.

8   *Ibid.*, 8.

9   Herring, "Emigration! Where to Go, and Wages," *After Work: A Magazine for Workmen's Homes*, vol. 1, January 1, 1874, 24.

10 McMurray, *The Free Grant Lands of Canada*, 16.

11 Toronto Public Library, "Local Flavour: Eating in Toronto, 1830–1955." *http://ve.torontopubliclibrary.ca/local_flavour/*

12 King, *Letters from Muskoka*, 23.

13 *Ibid.*, 24.

14 McMurray, *The Free Grant Lands of Canada*, 21.

15 James Boyer, "Muskoka History," *Muskoka Herald*, June 15, 1905.

16 Marshall, *The Canadian Dominion*, 51.

17 Murray, *Muskoka and Haliburton*, "Gravenhurst's Celebration of the Opening of the Railway," Orillia, *Times*, November 18, 1875, 352.

18 John Clay, *New World Notes*, 112.

Chapter Four

1   McMurray, *The Free Grant Lands of Canada*, 54.

2   Marshall, *The Canadian Dominion*, 59–60.

3   *Ibid.*, 64.

4   *Ibid.*, 65.

5   King, *Letters from Muskoka*, 34.

6   *The Ontario Farmer*, April 1869, 20.

7   Kirkwood and Murphy, *The Undeveloped Lands in Northern & Western Ontario*, 35.

8   Joseph Dale, *Canadian Land Grants in 1874*, 11.

9   Jane Tritton Gurney, "A Journey to Canada," *Cheltenham Ladies' College Magazine*, autumn 1887, 181.

10 In the original *English Bloods*, de la Fosse referred to Harston as Captain Martin; in a 2004 reprint of the book, editor Scott Shipman explained that de la Fosse had strived to keep identities hidden.

11 Frederick de la Fosse (published under pseudonym Roger Vardon), *English Bloods*, 59.

12 *Ibid.*, 49.

13 Thomas Osborne, *The Night the Mice Danced the Quadrille*, 18 (reissue of original untitled memoir).

14 Kirkwood and Murphy, *The Undeveloped Lands in Northern & Western Ontario*, 38.

15 Ontario, *Sessional Papers*, 36 Victoria 1872–73 (no. 12), 36.

16 Osborne, *The Night the Mice Danced the Quadrille*, 34.

17 King, *Letters from Muskoka*, 175.

18 Herring, *Emigration to the British Colonies*, 6.

19 W.E. Hamilton, *Muskoka Sketch*, 12.

20 Murray, *Muskoka and Haliburton*, "Canada, Special Commission ... to Investigate Indian Affairs in Canada, Report, 1858," 123.

21 *Ibid*, "Vernon B. Wadsworth's Reminiscences of Indians in Muskoka and Haliburton, 1860–4," 125.

22 Clay, *New World Notes*, 119.

23 King, *Letters from Muskoka*, 66.

24 Mrs. Copleston, *Canada: Why We Live in It, and Why We Like It*, 59.

25 *Ibid.*, 70.

26 James Boyer, "Muskoka History," *Muskoka Herald*, June 15, 1905.

27 King, *Letters from Muskoka*, 159.

28 Hamilton, *Muskoka Sketch*, 27.

29 William F. Munro, *The Backwoods' Life*, 12.

30 Gurney, "A Journey to Canada," 180.

31 From the Muskoka Collection, Bracebridge, Ontario, Public Library.

Chapter Five

1   Letter from Muskoka settler to Arthur Clayden, *Globe*, January 6, 1873.

2   Ontario, *Sessional Papers*, 34 Victoria 1870–71 (no. 28), Appendix B, 17.

3   *What Emigration Really Is* (anonymous), 5–6, 11.

4   Initially, I assumed this was Adelaide Street East, as that would have been in the vicinity of St. James Cathedral, where Herring might have stayed with clergy living nearby. However, in 1870, the Toronto city directory had Adelaide East stopping about ten house numbers short of 126. However, 126 Adelaide Street West, roughly at the corner of York and Adelaide, was the home of a John Bell, Q.C., barrister and solicitor. This seemed an unlikely place for Herring to stay, but an Internet search turned up an explanation. In a letter to the editor, published in the December 1, 1870, edition of the *Christian*, a London, England-based periodical, Herring mentioned John Bell, a barrister and solicitor, at that address, noting that Bell could give advice on investments in emigration. Somehow the two men had connected, and presumably Herring was Bell's guest when he stayed in Toronto.

5   Ontario, *Sessional Papers*, 34 Victoria 1870–71 (no. 28), 12.

6   John Morrison to Donald McLean, September 29, 1866. (From Marion Diamond, *Emigration and Empire: the Life of Maria S. Rye*, 166.)

7 Rye to McLean, January 17, 1867. (From Diamond, *Emigration and Empire*, 166.)

8 Allendale Grainger, *Charges Made Against Miss M. Rye, Before the Poor Law Board at Islington, and Her Reply Thereof (1874), Early Canadiana Online, http://www.canadiana.org/ECO/mtq?doc=07098*, 15.

9 John Joseph Kelso Papers (manuscript), Diary, 47.

10 William J. Patterson, *Some Plain Statements About Immigration, and Its Results*, 1.

11 *Ibid.*, 8.

12 Arthur Clayden, *Revolt of the Field*, 211.

13 This may sound unlikely, but I have compared portraits of both men, and in some there *is* a remarkable resemblance between them.

14 Clayden, *Revolt of the Field*, 217

15 *Ibid.*

16 *Ibid.*

17 *Ibid.*, 218.

18 Ontario, *Sessional Papers*, 36 Victoria 1873 (no. 18), 5.

Chapter Six

1 London *Times* editorial, August 21, 1874.

2 W.E. Hamilton had an amusing story about the Duke of Manchester's celebrity status in Bracebridge. The duke stayed at the British Lion, the town's finest hotel in Hamilton's opinion, and he reported, "The rumpling of the sheets the next morning showed that notwithstanding his exalted rank, he went to bed like ordinary commoners, and the couch was fondly glanced at, and shown to the curious, as a link joining Bracebridge to the House of Lords." (Hamilton, *Muskoka Sketch*, 17)

3 Hamilton, *Muskoka Sketch*, 17.

4 *Ibid.*, 16.

5 Geraldine Coombe, *The Muskoka Story*, 73.

6 Murray, *Muskoka and Haliburton*, "Visit of the Governor General," (Orillia *Times*, August 6, 1874), 407.

7 Lady Dufferin, *My Canadian Journal*, 162.

8 I have searched extensively for evidence that Herring left behind personal correspondence, but have found very little as of date of publication.

9 Herring, "Victoria Discussion Society," *Victoria Magazine*, January 1875, 205.

Chapter Seven

1 Clay, *New World Notes*, 112.

2 Patricia Jasen, *Wild Things: Nature, Culture, and Tourism in Ontario, 1790–1914*, 44. The entry for William Forsyth in the Dictionary of Canadian Biography Online reports a slightly different description of the animals, but none seemed overly "ferocious."

3 McMurray, *The Free Grant Lands of Canada*, 19.

4 The Icelandic volcano is actually named Hekla; apparently a spelling error altered its namesake's designation.

5 Clay, *New World Notes*, 118.

6 King, *Letters from Muskoka*, 155.

7 *Ibid.*, 268.

8 De la Fosse, *English Bloods*, 38–39.

9 *Ibid.*, 190.

10 Robert J. Boyer, *A Good Town Grew Here*, 28.

11 Hamilton, *Muskoka Sketch*, 28.

12 Boyer, *A Good Town Grew Here*, 28.

13 W.E. Hamilton, ed., *Guide Book & Atlas to Muskoka and Parry Sound*, 2.

14 *Ibid.*

15 *Ibid.*, 4.

16 *Ibid.*

Chapter Eight

1 Ontario, *Report of the Commissioners*, Appendix R, 13.

2 Ontario, *Report of the Commissioners*, 539.

3 For clarification: the main section of *Report of the Commissioners* was a commentary on the commissioners' actual report, which was published as Appendix R, which was included at the back of the book with other appendices.

4 Ontario, *Report of the Commissioners*, Appendix R, 21.

5 *Ibid.*, 13.

6 Ontario, *Report of the Commissioners*, 539

7 Ontario, *Report of the Commissioners*, Appendix R, 21.

8 Ontario, *Report of the Commissioners*, 542.

9 *Ibid.*

10 Hamilton, *Muskoka Sketch*, 35.

11 *Proceedings of the Royal Colonial Institute*, vol. 12, 238.

12 *Ibid.*, 239.

13 *Ibid.*, 238.

14 *Ibid.*

15 Herring, *Nearly Forty Years*, 38.

16 Information derived from the September 22, 1883, edition of the *Globe and Mail*.

17 Published in the *Globe*, June 8, 1885.

Chapter Nine

1 De la Fosse, *English Bloods*, 221.

2 Hamilton, *Muskoka Sketch*, 4.

3 King, *Letters from Muskoka*, 186.

4 *Ibid.*, 181.

5 Trent University Archives: *http://www2.trentu.ca/library/archives/92-1007.htm.*

6 De la Fosse, *English Bloods*, 219.

7 *Ibid.*, 220.

8 Hamilton, *Peeps at My Life*, 11.

9 P.A.,Wayman, "Peeps at William Edwin Hamilton," *Irish Astronomical Society*, January 1999, 71.

10 Hamilton, *Peeps at My Life*, 49.

11 Herring's "We have got the ships…" must have been inspired by the music hall song written and composed by G.W. Hunt in 1878 and sung by the popular performer G.H. Macdermott. The song was known as Macdermott's War Song and started with "We don't want to fight but by jingo if we do/We've got the ships, we've got the men, and got the money too!"

Epilogue

1 McMurray, *The Free Grant Lands of Canada*, 56.

Bibliography

Primary Sources

Bate, John. *Emigration: Free, Assisted and Full-Paying Passages: Together with the Conditions for Obtaining Free Land Grants, Rules for Emigration Clubs, &c.* London: Cassell, Petter, and Galpin, [187–?].

Biograph and Review. "Rev. A. Styleman Herring, M.A." Vol. 5, 607–611. London: E.W. Allen, 1881.

Boyer, James. "Muskoka History." *Muskoka Herald.* June 15, 1905.

Burdett, Henry C. "The Sanitary Institute of Great Britain." *The Sanitary Record: A Journal of Public Health.* Vol. 9, July–December, 1868, 264. London: Smith, Elder & Co., 1879.

Clay, John. *New World Notes: Being an Account of Journeyings and Sojournings in America and Canada.* Kelso (Scotland): J. & J.H. Rutherford, 1875.

Clayden, Arthur. *Revolt of the Field.* London: Hodder and Stoughton, 1874.

Copleston, Mrs. Edward. *Canada: Why We Live in It, and Why We Like It.* London: Parker, Son, and Bourn, 1861.

Dale, Joseph. *Canadian Land Grants in 1874.* London: Edward Stanford, 1875.

Dufferin and Ava, Marchioness of (Lady Dufferin). *My Canadian Journal 1872-8*. London: John Murray, 1891.

Fosse, Frederick de la [Roger Vardon, pseudo.]. *English Bloods*. Ottawa: Graphic Publishers, 1930. [Reprinted as *English Bloods: In the Backwoods of Muskoka, 1878*. Ed., Scott D. Shipman. Toronto: Natural Heritage Books, 2004.

Foy, Charles. *Emigration or No Emigration: Facts for Emigrants*. Belfast: W. & G. Baird, 1874.

____. *Emigration to Canada*. Monaghan (Ireland): Northern Standard, [1872?].

French, T. P. *Information for Intending Settlers on the Ottawa and Opeongo Road, And Its Vicinity*. Ottawa, Canada West, 1857.

Grainger, Allendale. *Charges Made Against Miss M. Rye, Before the Poor Law Board at Islington, and Her Reply Thereto*. [1874?].

A Guidebook Containing Information for Intending Settlers. Ottawa: Department of Agriculture, 1883.

Gurney, Jane Tritton. "A Journey to Canada, 1887." *Cheltenham Ladies' College Magazine*. Autumn, 1887, 177–87. Cheltenham Ladies' College: Cheltenham, Eng.

Hamilton, W. E. *Guide Book & Atlas of Muskoka and Parry Sound Districts*. Toronto: H.R. Page, 1879.

____. *Muskoka Sketch*. Dresden, Ont.: Times Printing Co., 1884.

____. *Peeps at My Life*, 2nd ed. Chatham, Ont.: Banner Printing Co., 1895.

Hand and Heart: The Church Herald and Review. Vol. 6, no. 291, Friday, July 29, 1881.

Herring, A. Styleman. *Emigration for Poor Folks*. London: S. W. Partridge & Co., 1869.

____. *Emigration to the British Colonies by the Clerkenwell Emigration Society*. London: Gilbert and Rivington, printers, 1870.

____. "Emigration! Where to Go, and Wages." *After Work: A Magazine for Workmen's Homes*. Vol. 1, January 1, 1874, 22–24. London: William Macintosh.

____. *Letters From Abroad, With Hints to Emigrants Proceeding to the New Dominion of Canada*. London: S.W. Partridge & Co., 1871.

____. *Nearly Forty Years Exclusively Among the Poor of London*. London: J.W. Poulton, 1896.

____. "Victoria Discussion Society," *Victoria Magazine*. Vol. 24, January 1875, 189–207. London: Victoria Press.

Hobart, Lady. *Help for the Helpless: London's Bitter Cry Hushed in Canada*. London: John F. Shaw and Co., 1884.

Jenkins, Edward. *Canadian Immigration in 1875: Report to the Honorable the Minister of Agriculture, upon the position and prospects of immigration, and with comparative statements of emigration from Great Britain during the past four years*. Montreal: Dawson Brothers, 1876.

____. *State Emigration: An Essay*. London: Edward Stanford, 1869.

Kelso, John Joseph. Papers, "Scrapbook of newspaper clippings concerning child emigration to Canada." Thomas Fisher Rare Book Library, University of Toronto.

King, Harriet Barbara. *Letters From Muskoka by an Emigrant Lady*. London: Richard Bentley and Son, 1878.

Kirkwood, Alexander and Joseph J. Murphy. *The Undeveloped Lands in Northern & Western Ontario*. Toronto: Hunter, Rose & Co., 1878.

MacDermott, Charles Landy. *Facts for Emigrants: A Journey from London to the Backwoods of Canada*. London: H. Born, 1868.

Marshall, Charles. *The Canadian Dominion*. London: Longmans, Green, and Co., 1871.

McMurray, Thomas. *The Free Grant Lands of Canada, From Practical Experience of Bush Farming in the Free Grant Districts of Muskoka and Parry Sound*. Bracebridge, Ont.: Northern Advocate, 1871.

_____. *Temperance Lectures*. Toronto: Hunter, Rose & Company, 1873.

Munro, William F. *The Backwoods' Life*. Toronto: Hunter, Rose & Co., 1869.

Nelson, Joseph. *Emigration to North Americas: A Letter to the Right Honourable G.J. Goschen, M.P., President of the Poor Law Board*. London: Abbot, Barton & Co., 1869.

Ontario Farmer. "Roughing It in the Bush." Vol. 1, 4: 120. April 1869. Toronto: Hunter, Rose & Co.

Osborne, Thomas. *The Night the Mice Danced the Quadrille: Five Years in the Backwoods*. Reprint of unpublished manuscript. Erin, Ont.: Stoddart, Boston Mills Press, 1995.

Patterson, William J. *Some Plain Statements About Immigration, and Its Results*. [Ottawa?]: [1872?]. Submitted at the annual meeting of the Dominion Board of Trade.

Proceedings of the Royal Colonial Institute, 1880–81, vol. 12. Royal Commonwealth Society. London: Sampson Low, Marston, Searle & Rivington, 1881.

Rye, Maria S. *What the People Say About the Children and What the Children Say About Canada*. London: Jas. Wade (printer), 1871.

Smiles, Samuel. *Self-Help*. London: John Murray, 1866.

Torrens, Robert R. *Two Speeches of Robert R. Torrens, Esq., M.P., on Emigration and the Colonies*. London: Cornelius Buck, [1870?].

Torrens, William McCullagh. *Imperial and Colonial Partnership in Emigration*. London: Edward Stanford, [1881?].

What Emigration Really Is, by a Resident in Canada and Australia. London: The Graphotying Co., Ltd., [1870?].

White, Thomas. *A Lecture on Canada as a Field for Emigration: With Special reference to the Inducements offered by the Government of the Province of Ontario*. Toronto: Hunter, Rose & Co., 1869.

Secondary Sources

Boyer, George White. *Early Days in Muskoka: A Story About the Settlement of Communities in the Free Grant Lands and of Pioneer Life in Muskoka.* Bracebridge, Ont.: Herald-Gazette Press, 1970.

Boyer, James. "Muskoka History." *Muskoka Herald.* June 15, 1905.

Boyer, Robert J. *Early Exploration and Surveying of Muskoka District, Ontario, Canada.* Bracebridge, Ont.: Herald-Gazette Press, 1979.

____. *A Good Town Grew Here: The Story of Bracebridge.* 2nd ed. Bracebridge, Ont.: Oxbow Press, 2002.

Bray, Carolyn. "The Domino Effect." *Muskoka Magazine.* October/November 2004, 57–62.

Brown, Enid. *Stephenson Township: Its Founders and Early Church Life 1868–1957.* Utterson, Ont: Woman's Association of Utterson United Church, 1958.

Coombe, Geraldine. *Muskoka Past and Present.* Toronto: McGraw-Hill Ryerson, 1976.

Cowan, Helen I. *British Emigration to British North America: The First Hundred Years.* Revised edition. Toronto: University of Toronto Press, 1961.

Diamond, Marion. *Emigration and Empire: The Life of Maria S. Rye.* New York: Garland Publishing Inc., 1999.

Dunae, Patrick A. "Promoting the Dominion: Records and the Canadian Immigration Campaign, 1872–1915." *Archivaria 19.* Winter 1984–85, 73–93.

Evans, A. Margaret. "The Mowat Era, 1872–1896: Stability and Progress." *Profiles of a Province: Studies in the History of Ontario.* Edith G. Firth (ed.), 97–106. Toronto: Ontario Historical Society, 1967.

Forman, Debra (ed.). *Legislators and Legislatures of Ontario: A Reference Guide.* Vol. 2. Toronto: Ontario Legislative Library, Research and Information Services, 1984.

Gates, Lillian. *Land Policies of Upper Canada*. Toronto: University of Toronto Press, 1968.

Glazebrook, G. P. deT. *Life in Ontario: A Social History*. Toronto: University of Toronto Press, 1968.

Grainger, Brett. "The Other Muskoka." *Toronto Life*. July 2005, 50–57.

Harper, Marjory. "Enticing the Emigrant: Canadian Agents in Ireland and Scotland, c. 1870–c. 1920," *Scottish Historical Review*. Vol. 83, 1: no. 215, April 2004, 41–58.

Heritage Muskoka: Notes on the History of Muskoka District as Presented by Guest Speakers on Behalf of Georgian College. Parry Sound: Algonquin Regional Library System, 1976.

Hoffman, Douglas W. and Henry F. Noble. *Acreages of Soil Capability Classes for Agriculture in Ontario*. Toronto: Rural Development Branch, Ontario Ministry of Agriculture and Food. Ottawa: Department of Regional Economic Expansion, 1975.

Jasen, Patricia. *Wild Things: Nature, Culture, and Tourism in Ontario 1790–1914*. Toronto: University of Toronto Press, 1995.

Kohli, Marjorie. *The Golden Bridge: Young Immigrants to Canada, 1833–1959*. Toronto: Natural Heritage Books, 2003.

Ladell, John L. *They Left Their Mark: Surveyors and Their Role in the Settlement of Ontario*. Toronto: Dundurn Press, 1993.

Malchow, Howard L. *Population Pressures: Emigration and Government in Late Nineteenth-Century Britain*. Palo Alto, California: Society for the Promotion of Science and Scholarship, 1979.

Markey, D. *More a Symbol than a Success: Foundation Years of the Swan River Colony*. Bayswater, Australia: Westbooks, 1977.

Murray, Florence B. "Agricultural Settlement on the Canadian Shield: Ottawa to Georgian Bay." *Profiles of a Province: Studies in the History of Ontario*. Edith G. Firth, ed., 178–186. Toronto: Ontario Historical Society, 1967.

_____. ed., *Muskoka and Haliburton 1615-1875: A Collection of Documents*. Toronto: The Champlain Society for the Government of Ontario, University of Toronto Press, 1963.

Pryke, Susan. *Huntsville: With Spirit and Resolve*. Huntsville, Ont.: Fox Meadow Creations, 2000.

_____. *Explore Muskoka*. Reprint of 1987 edition. Erin, Ont.: Boston Mills Press, 1999.

Richards, Eric. *Britannia's Children: Emigration From England, Scotland, Wales and Ireland Since 1600*. London: Hambledon and London, 2004.

Richards, J. Howard. "Lands and Policies: Attitudes and Controls in the Alienation of Lands in Ontario During the First Century of Settlement." *Ontario History*. Vol. 50, autumn 1958. Toronto: Ontario Historical Society, 193–209.

_____. "Land Use and Settlement Patterns on the Fringe of the Shield in Southern Ontario." University of Toronto Ph.D. thesis, 1954.

Spragge, George W. "Colonization Roads in Canada West, 1850–67." *Ontario History*. Vol. 49, winter 1957. Toronto: Ontario Historical Society, 1–17.

Wayman, P. A. "Peeps at William Edwin Hamilton." *Irish Astronomical Journal*. January 1999, vol. 26 (1), 69–72.

Wood, J. David. *Making Ontario: Agricultural Colonization and Landscape Re-creation Before the Railway*. Montreal: McGill-Queen's University Press, 2000.

Government Documents

Canada: *Census*, 1931

_____. "First Report of the Select Committee of the Parliament of Canada on Immigration and Colonisation." *Journals, House of Commons of Canada*. Vol. 9, 1875.

Ontario, *Emigration to Canada: The Province of Ontario: Its Soil, Climate, Resources, Institutions, Free Grant Lands, &c., &c.* Toronto: Department of Agriculture, 1869, 1871, 1874.

_____. *Ministry of Tourism and Recreation*, Tourism Profiles for Ontario Regions. n.d.

_____. *Report of the Commissioners.* Toronto: Agricultural Commission, 1881.

_____. *Sessional Papers.* n.d.

Statistics Canada, *Agricultural Community Profile.* Muskoka, 2006.

Archives

Archives of Ontario.

Bracebridge, Ontario, Public Library, Muskoka Collection.

Huntsville, Ontario, Public Library.

Websites

Gryffyn Lodge. *http://www.gryffinlodge.ca.*

Historical Glimpses of Stephenson Township. Stephenson Township Post Offices. *http://home.primus.ca/~robkath/indsteph.htm.* (Accessed in 2003. Unavailable at time of writing.)

Immigrants to Canada. "Emigration Information of the Nineteenth Century." *http://retirees.uwaterloo.ca/~marj/genealogy/thevoyage.html.*

Library and Archives Canada. "Exploration and Settlement: Moving Here, Staying Here: The Canadian Immigrant Experience." *District of Muskoka Settler's Guide. http://www.collectionscanada.gc.ca/immigrants/021017-2000-e.html.*

Muskoka Farm Fresh. *http://www.muskokafarmfresh.com.*

National Library of Australia. "Australia Trove." *http://trove.nla.gov.au.*

19th Century British Library Newspapers Database. *http://www.bl.uk/ reshelp/findhelprestype/news/newspdigproj/database/index.html.*

19th Century U.S. Newspapers. *http://gdc.gale.com/products/19th-century- u.s.-newspapers.*

Paper of Record. *https://paperofrecord.hypernet.ca/default.asp.*

Savour Muskoka. *http://www.savourmuskoka.com.*

Toronto Public Library. "Local Flavour: Eating in Toronto, 1830–1955." *http://ve.torontopubliclibrary.ca/local_flavour.*

Trent University Archives. Fonds Level Description. "De la Fosse, F. M., 1859–1950." *http://www2.trentu.ca/library/archives/92-1007.htm.*

Windermere House. *http://www.windermerehouse.com.*

Index

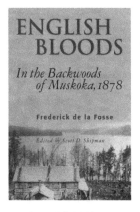

English Bloods
In the Backwoods of Muskoka, 1878
Frederick de la Fosse, Scott D. Shipman (Ed.)
9781896219967
$24.95

Farming in the Canadian backwoods in the late 1800s was a prospect that enticed many young Englishmen to cross the Atlantic. One such fellow was Frederick de la Fosse, whose well-meaning uncle paid £100 per annum for his young nephew to serve as a farm pupil in the northern reaches of Muskoka. Some years later, de la Fosse, under the pseudonym of Roger Vardon, wrote an illuminating and humorous biographical account of the trials and tribulations of the "English Bloods," the local epithet attached to these young lads attempting to hone farming skills in a land never intended to be agricultural. And, in so doing, de la Fosse chronicles the realities of pioneer life in the area.

In the original text, published in 1930, a number of names were changed to conceal identities of the local people. Editor Scott D. Shipman has spent over eight years researching the authentic names and overall background for this new augmented edition of *English Bloods*. The richly descriptive text written by the keenly observant and erudite de la Fosse is complemented by archival visuals and annotations for today's reader.

Frederick de la Fosse went on to become a public librarian in Peterborough in 1910.

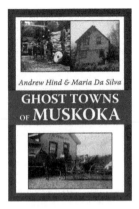

Ghost Towns of Muskoka
Andrew Hind and Maria Da Silva
9781550027969
$24.99

Ghost Towns of Muskoka explores the tragic history of a collection of communities from across Muskoka whose stars have long since faded. Today, these ghost towns are merely a shadow — or spectre — of what they once were. Some have disappeared entirely, having been swallowed by regenerating forests, while others have been reduced to foundations, forlorn buildings, and silent ruins. A few support a handful of inhabitants, but even these towns are wrapped in a ghostly shroud.

But this book isn't only about communities that have died. Rather it is about communities that lived, vibrantly at that, if only for a brief time. It's about the people whose dreams for a better life these villages represented; the people who lived, loved, laboured, and ultimately died in these small wilderness settlements. And it's about an era in history, those early heady days of Muskoka settlement when the forests were flooded with loggers and land-hungry settlers.

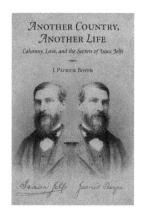

Another Country, Another Life
Calumny, Love, and the Secrets of Isaac Jelfs
J. Patrick Boyer
9781459708402
$24.99

James Boyer's impressive life story — editor of the first newspaper in Ontario's northern districts, homesteading farmer, schoolteacher, town clerk of Bracebridge for many decades, Methodist choir director, and Muskoka district magistrate from 1878 to 1900 — is well documented in books and newspaper features. Behind his noteworthy Canadian life, however, lurked the haunting shadow of another past.

Isaac Jelfs, a young English clerk, found himself scapegoat for a Stratford law office scandal soon after his career began. Escaping to Birmingham, the desperate Jelfs married, then joined the Dragoon Guards in the Crimean War. After witnessing the bloody chaos of the battlefield, Jelfs deserted and immigrated to New York, where he fell in love with another woman. Soon they fled to Canada with their love child in tow. Once across the border, Jelfs began to create his new life — as a Muskoka pioneer named James Boyer.

Great White Fleet
Celebrating Canada Steamship Lines
Passenger Ships
John Henry
9781459710467
$30.00

For decades Canada Steamship Lines pro-
claimed itself as the world's largest transportation company operating on inland waters. Its
passenger and freight vessels could be found on the Great Lakes as far west
as Duluth, Minnesota, and as far east as the Lower St. Lawrence River.

The passenger steamers were known collectively as the Great White
Fleet. These ships — from day-excursion vessels to well-appointed cruise
ships — had rich histories. The sheer scope of these passenger services
were a wonder to behold. No fewer than 51 steamers comprised the passenger fleet at the company's inception in 1913, and its network of routes
was awesome.

This is the story of the beloved steamers of the Great White Fleet
from 1913–65, when the passenger vessels stopped running. Nearly half
a century after the last passenger boats sailed, this book will provide a
window into a wonderful lost way of life.

Available at your favourite bookseller.

 DUNDURN

Visit us at
Dundurn.com
@dundurnpress
Facebook.com/dundurnpress
Pinterest.com/dundurnpress